What people have said about Mike Baxter's previous books

Core Values

... and how they underpin strategy & organisational culture

Featuring academic research, business case studies and
analysis of the strategies of 36 UK universities

Mike Baxter

Goal Atlas Ltd

First published by Goal Atlas Ltd, Isleworth, UK.

British Library Cataloguing-in-Publication Data: A catalogue record for this book is available from the British Library.

ISBN: 978-1-8382760-7-2

To Cathy, my wife, editor, publisher
and all-too-often under-acknowledged
contributor to everything I produce.

Contents

Executive Summary	1
About Mike Baxter	3
About Goal Atlas	4
Part 1 Setting the Scene	7
The basics of core values	8
Introducing the Core Values Framework	11
Introducing the Core Values Workflow	13
Part 2 The Core Values Framework	17
Which core values?	18
Types of core values	18
Explicitly articulate core values	22
How many core values?	23
Most frequent core values	24
Make core values matter	26
Presentation formats for core values	28
Clarifying intended impact of core values	31
What next, after core values?	32
How values and strategy fit together	35
Core values and organisational culture	38
Part 3 The Core Values Workflow	49
Core Values Workflow	51
Scope core values	53
Devise / revise core values	63
Articulate & apply core values	71
Track & refine core values	80
Concluding remarks	85
References	87
Appendix 1: University values research	91
Appendix 2: Lists of values	96

MIKE BAXTER

Executive Summary

My hope, in writing this book, is to provide a short, highly accessible and practical guide for anyone interested in making core values impactful for an organisation.

In a turbulent and fast changing world, leaders of organisations of all sizes and sorts are desperately seeking anchors – firm, enduring points of reference from which to triangulate their plans, decisions and actions.

Core values can provide such anchorage and can do so in ways conducive to empowering leadership, employee engagement, participative governance and purposeful work.

To make a difference with core values is, however, no quick win, as research, discussed in this book, has shown. To have any significant impact, core values need to affect the lived experience of people both inside and outside the organisation.

This book sets out to enable leaders to:

- Think more deeply and more systematically about core values;
- Discuss core values more meaningfully and perceptively;
- Decide on core values more rigorously;
- Present and apply core values more impactfully.

In general, the aim here is to have core values feature more prominently and more usefully in the life of your organisation. By doing so, core values can provide a robust foundation for impactful strategy and strong organisational culture.

At the heart of this book are two interconnected ideas. The first is a way of making sense of core values – the **Core Values Framework**. This sets out the basics of core values (what they are and what they are for) and provides a way of categorising them to help you decide which values are best suited to your organisation. The Framework then explains how to make core values matter and how to embed them into ways of working via people strategy and organisational culture.

The second idea is how to work with core values – the **Core Values Workflow**. The Workflow begins with scoping. To scope core values means to determine what they mean for an organisation and what they are going to be used for. It clarifies what it means to say core values are fit-for-purpose. Then Workflow goes on to devise core values, articulate and apply them and finally track and refine them.

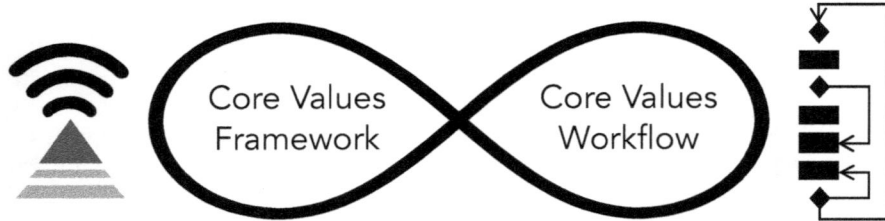

To make this book more practical and to enrich the context in which these ideas are discussed, the strategies of 36 UK universities were analysed to see how they presented their core values (Appendix 1). UK universities make great real-world examples because of their tradition of publishing their strategy documents, most of which contain statements of their core values. This, it is hoped, will provide a valuable cross-fertilisation of thinking, sharing learnings from the commercial world with leaders of UK universities and sharing the published strategies of the university sector with commercial leaders.

This book is written in three parts. The first part is a very brief overview of the book and orientation to its contents. Quickly review this part to get a feel for what comes next. Then you can decide what you and your organisation needs most. If you want to make better sense of values, dive straight into Part 2. If on the other hand you want to be able to work with core values better (devising them, articulating them, applying them or tracking their impact), jump straight into Part 3.

About Mike Baxter

Dr Mike Baxter has been awarded a PhD in Science, a personal Professorship and Chartered Designer status. He has been a business consultant since 2001, delivering over 10,000 hours of consultancy to the leadership of some of the world's biggest brands, including Cisco, Google, HSBC, Lilly, Skype and Sony PlayStation. With a background in psychology and design, he has been an advisor to both the UK government and to some of London's fastest growing tech start-ups. Mike is a recognised specialist in the field of strategy and is the author of *The Strategy Manual: A step-by-step guide to the transformational change of anything.*

As a former Professor & Dean of Ravensbourne University and Director of Brunel University's Design Research Centre, Mike has an extensive background in Higher Education (HE). He advises Vice-Chancellors and the leadership teams of UK universities and has been a facilitator and speaker for HE bodies, such as UUK, HESPA, and the Russell Group Directors of Strategy. His independent research into the strategies of 52 UK universities was published as a benchmarking report, *University Strategy 2020*.

The organisations Mike has worked with...

...and the books he has distilled his experience into.

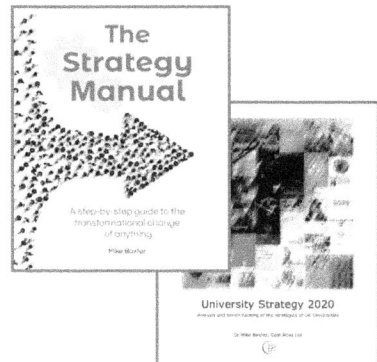

About Goal Atlas

Mike's company, Goal Atlas Ltd, was established in 2014 to work with leaders and teams, across sectors, to facilitate the systematic, hands-on production, management and governance of effective strategies. Goal Atlas undertakes consultancy and independent research into strategy and offers models and frameworks to enable strategy to be better adopted and more impactful within organisations.

Goal Atlas also publishes Mike's regular monthly newsletter, Strategy Distilled, offering a unique blend of insight, observations and learning for anyone who works on strategy, works with strategy or just loves strategy. Strategy Distilled is available to read or listen to as a podcast via a free subscription and on the Goal Atlas website.

STRATEGY
DISTILLED

Goal Atlas
goalatlas.com

Part 1 Setting the Scene

The basics of core values
What are values?

Definition of core values

Features of core values

What core values are not

What core values are for

Introducing the Core Values Framework
A framework for thinking about,

and making sense of, core values

Introducing the Core Values Workflow
A process to help you devise, communicate

and refine your organisation's core values

The basics of core values

What are values, in general?

The concept of 'value/s' can be used in different ways, for example:

1. Value can be a measure of the worth, importance or usefulness of an organisation to its customers, employees, suppliers or shareholders.

2. Values can be principles or beliefs that can help individuals make specific decisions in particular situations.

3. Values can be generic or enduring across an organisation, in which case they should help everyone make decisions repeatedly in many different situations. It is these that we call 'core values'.

What are organisational core values

Patrick Lencioni (2002) suggests that there are three types of organisational values. **Core values**, which are deeply ingrained principles that guide all of an organisation's actions, are sacrosanct and can never be compromised. **Aspirational values**, which the organisation doesn't have currently but are needed for success in the future. **Permission-to-play values**, which are the minimum behavioral and social standards required of any employee.

Whilst these may be useful distinctions for your organisation, they are too fine-grained for the purposes of this book, where we will refer simply to 'core values' as the shared principles and beliefs which guide the decisions and actions of everyone across the organisation. In other words, all values that are shared across the organisation will be called core values (i.e. they are core to the entire organisation) regardless of whether they are deeply ingrained, aspirational or minimum standards.

Definition of core values

Core values are the shared principles and beliefs which guide the decisions and actions of everyone across the organisation.

The basics of core values

Features of core values

Schwartz (1994) suggests that each core value:

1. "is a belief ...

2. that pertains to desirable end states or modes of conduct;

3. that transcends specific situations;

4. that guides selection or evaluation of behavior, people, and events and

5. that is ordered by importance relative to other values to form a system of value priorities."

What core values are NOT

'Core values' should never be a constraint on innovation, a prohibition on dissent or a mandate for unquestioning compliance.

The 'core values' of an organisation are NOT the personal values of the CEO.

'Core values' are not intended to dictate the personal values of individuals within organisations.

'Core values' are not a means of eliminating diversity in the workplace.

What core values are for

1. By guiding the decisions and actions of everyone across the organisation, core values simplify and streamline the way work is done, in uncertain circumstances, making the organisation more effective overall.

2. By having many people across an organisation working with shared beliefs and principles, their actions will tend to be more aligned.

3. An organisation operating on shared principles and beliefs will feel more of a community and will feel a stronger sense of purpose.

Core Values Framework

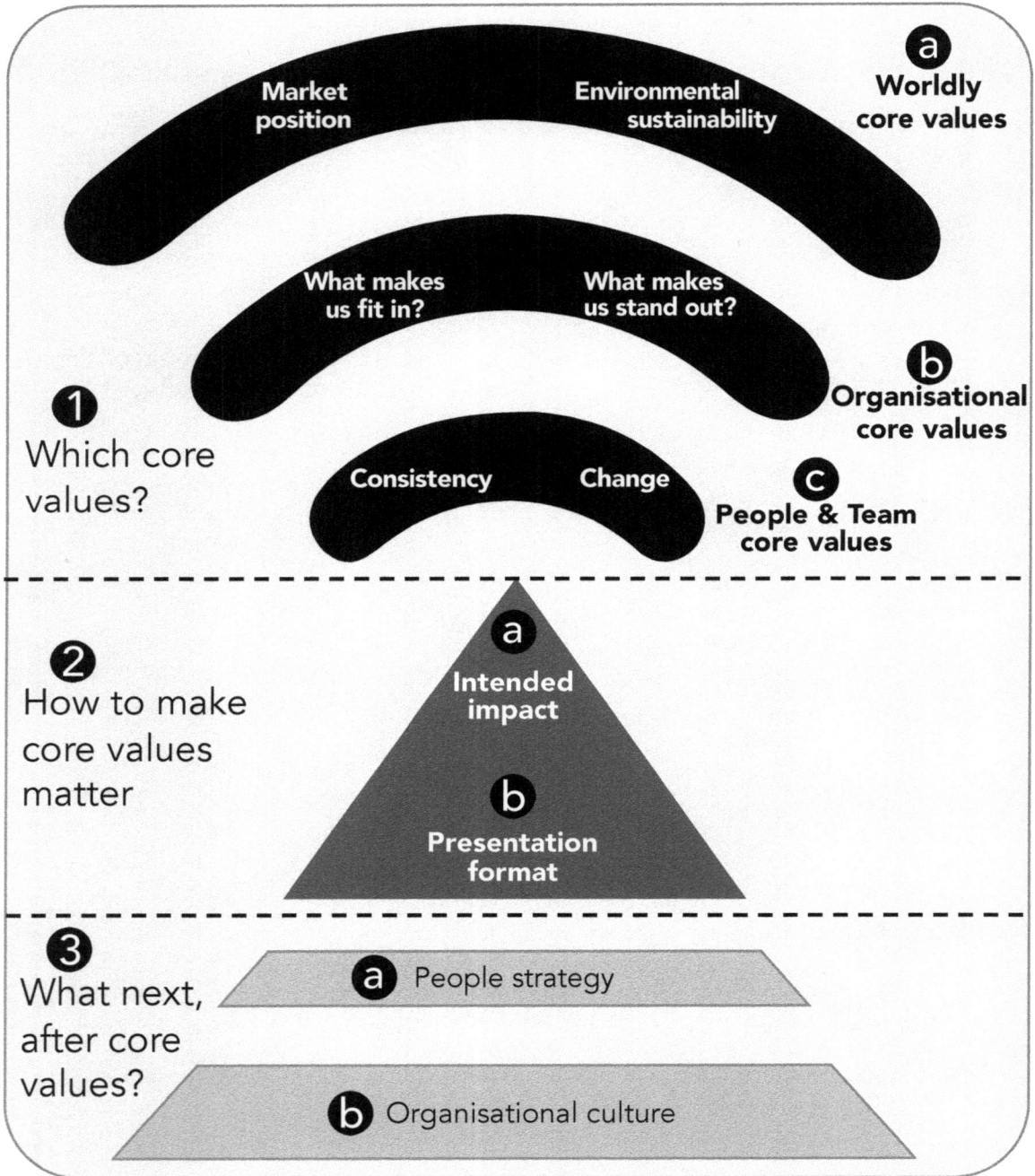

ⓐ Worldly core values

Market position

Environmental sustainability

What makes us fit in?

What makes us stand out?

ⓑ Organisational core values

Consistency

Change

ⓒ People & Team core values

❶ Which core values?

❷ How to make core values matter

ⓐ Intended impact

ⓑ Presentation format

❸ What next, after core values?

ⓐ People strategy

ⓑ Organisational culture

Introducing the Core Values Framework

The Core Values Framework helps you think about, and make sense of, core values so that, of all the values you could hold, you can identify, present and utilise those that will drive your organisation. The Core Values Framework has three elements:

1 **Which core values?** There are three distinct types of values shaping this decision:

a **Worldly core values.** Which values reflect how we see ourselves in the world? For example, values about market positioning or our stance on the climate crisis.

b **Organisational core values.** Which values reflect the kind of organisation we are, or aspire to be? Some of these may be defining or characteristic of the type of organisation we are (e.g. charity, tech startup). What makes us fit in with 'our' type of organisation? By contrast, we might want our values to reflect our distinctiveness. What makes us stand out from other organisations like us?

c **People and Team core values.** Which values affect the decisions and action of people and teams across the organisation? This is where the rubber hits the road for core values. This is where they have their most direct and tangible impact. These people and team values are typically intended to maintain consistency or to motivate change.

2 **How to make core values matter.** If core values are going to impact ways of working significantly across the organisation, their intended impact needs to be clear and they need to be compelling in their presentation.

a **Intended impact.** What are core values intended to change within your organisation? What impact are they intended to have?

b **Presentation format.** How core values are presented needs to be appropriate to the particular type of impact they are designed to have. A much more narrow presentational issue is the brevity and specificity of the description of each value. Are they merely one-word labels or are they detailed accounts of what each value means and how it should be acted upon?

3 **What next, after core values?** Once we've decided upon them and chosen how to present them, what then? What is underpinned by these core values? Typically core values will **a** sit at the heart of **people strategy** and **b** help shape **organisational culture**.

The Core Values Framework is described in more detail in Part 2.

Core Values Workflow

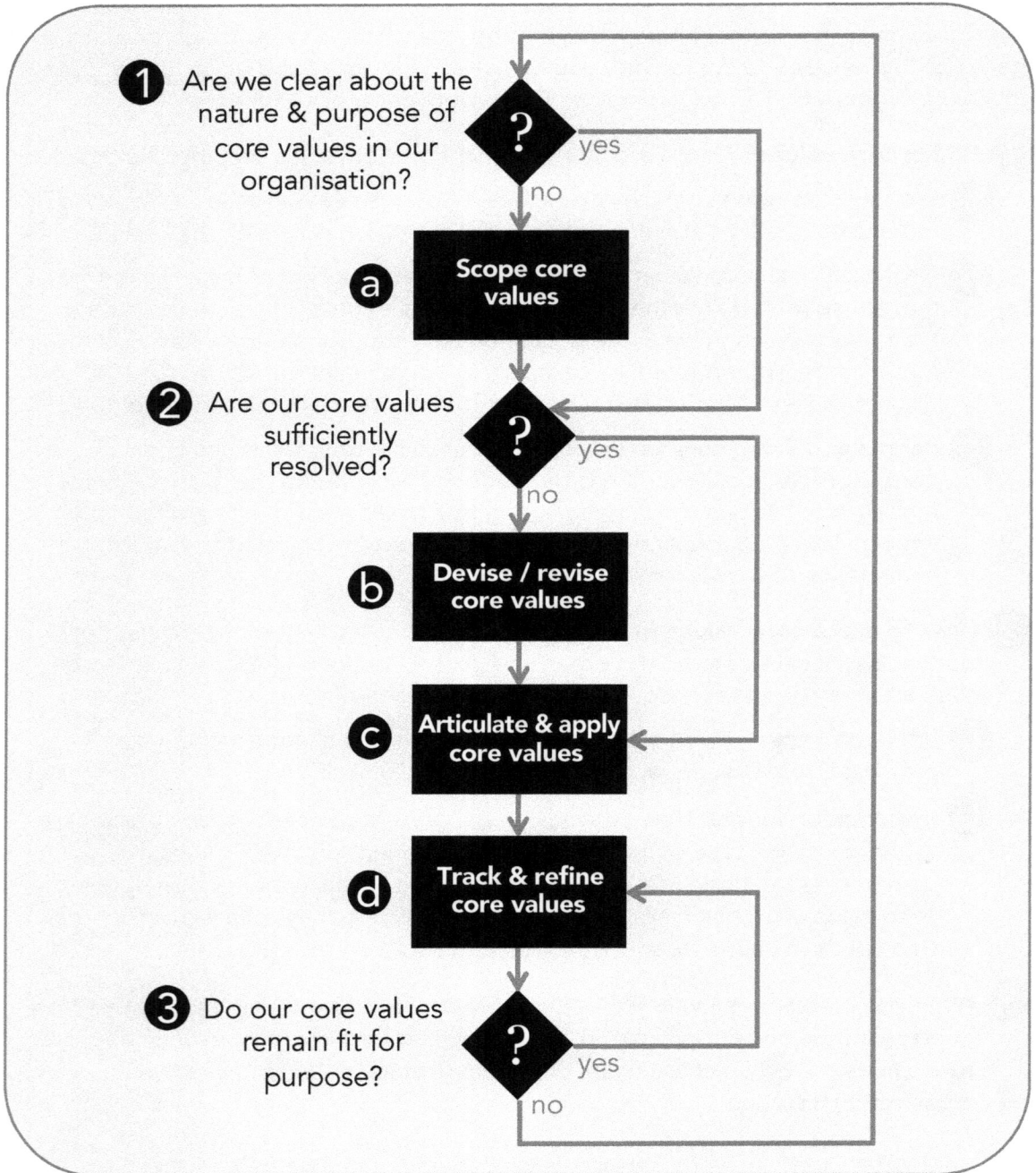

1 Are we clear about the nature & purpose of core values in our organisation? **?** yes / no

a Scope core values

2 Are our core values sufficiently resolved? **?** yes / no

b Devise / revise core values

c Articulate & apply core values

d Track & refine core values

3 Do our core values remain fit for purpose? **?** yes / no

Introducing the Core Values Workflow

The Core Values Workflow is the process by which you devise, communicate and refine your organisation's core values. It comprises three decision-making points (1-3) and four processes (a-d):

1 If you are unclear about the nature and purpose of core values in your organisation, a scoping process should be undertaken.

a This scoping process will determine: the extent to which your organisation already has core values; the intended audience for your core values (leaders, employees, suppliers, customers?); the purpose your core values are intended to serve.

2 Once scoping is complete, you need to decide if your core values are sufficiently resolved.

b The next process devises or revises your core values. This begins by reviewing existing core values and surfacing values that are implicit within the organisation.

c Next, your chosen core values need to be articulated and applied. How you articulate them will have a big influence on how they will be received and acted upon. How they are seen to be 'lived' inside the organisation, particularly how they are modelled and demonstrated by leadership, will have a big effect on the impact they make.

d Finally, core values need to be tracked, reviewed and periodically refined.

3 As part of the review and refine process, the final decision to be made is whether or not your chosen core values remain fit for purpose.

The Core Values Workflow is described in more detail in Part 3.

" To make your values mean something …

1. understand the different types of values,

2. be aggressively authentic and

3. own the process "

Patrick Lencioni (2002)

Words of wisdom on core values

"If you don't stick to your values when they're being tested, they're not values: they're hobbies."

Jon Stewart,
Host
The Daily Show

"It's not hard to make decisions, once you know what your values are"

Roy Disney,
Co-founder
Disney

"One of our values is that you should be looking out for each other. Everyone should try to make the lives of everyone else who works here a little bit simpler."

Stewart Butterfield,
Founder
Slack

"A key part of maintaining a great culture is the constant focus on the behaviors and values that best define it. We [Spotify] understand what our culture is and we live true to it."

Brittany Forsyth,
VP Human Relations
Spotify

"The culture of a workplace - an organization's values, norms and practices - has a huge impact on our happiness and success."

Adam Grant,
Professor
Wharton

"Your personal core values define who you are, and a company's core values ultimately define the company's character and brand. For individuals, character is destiny. For organizations, culture is destiny."

Tony Hsieh,
Founder
Zappos

Part 2 The Core Values Framework

Which core values?
Types of core values
Explicitly articulate core values
How many core values?
Most frequent core values

How to make core values matter
Presentation formats for core values
Clarifying intended impact of core values

What next, after core values?
How values and strategy fit together
Core values and organisational culture

Which core values?
Types of core values

At the top of our Core Values Framework on page 10 is this categorisation of different types of core values. '**Worldly core values**' are the broad sweeping values defining how we see our place in the world. '**Organisational core values**' give rise to the type of values that define our organisational identity – how we see ourselves as an organisation. '**People & Team core values**' give rise to values reflecting how we would wish our people and teams to see themselves and conduct themselves within our organisation.

Each of these types of core values will be explored in the sections that follow.

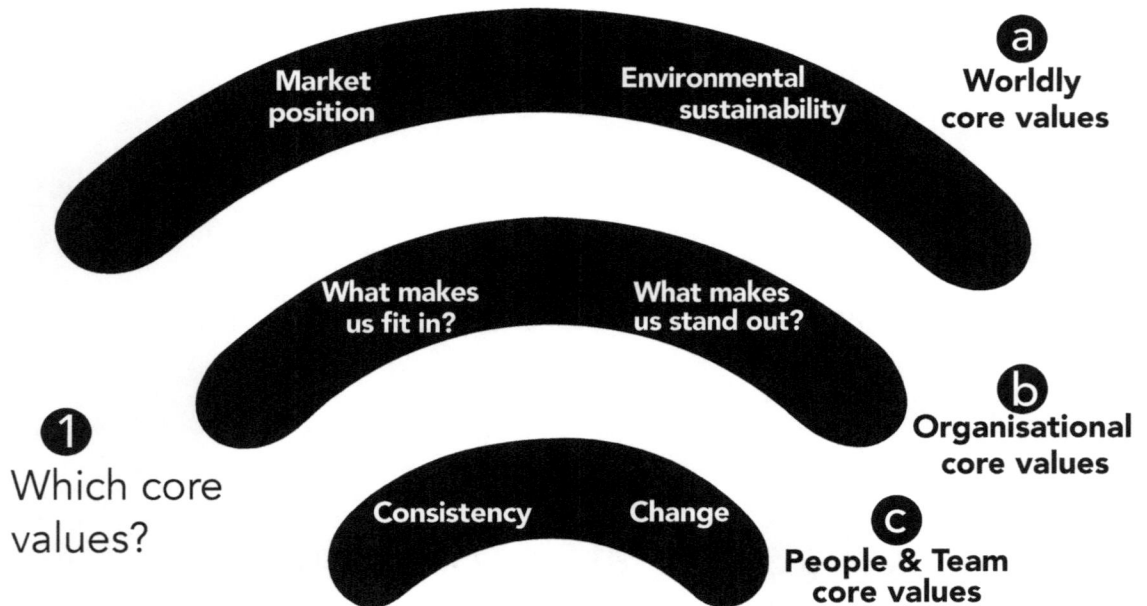

Market position

Environmental sustainability

a Worldly core values

What makes us fit in?

What makes us stand out?

b Organisational core values

1 Which core values?

Consistency

Change

c People & Team core values

'Worldly' core values

Worldly core values
Organisational core values
People & Team core values

Worldly core values. What values could we come up with to reflect how we see our organisation's place in the world? These will be the broadest and likely the most sweeping of our values. For most organisations there are two drivers of worldly core values: financial and non-financial. The financial drivers may be about profit or merely financial sustainability. The non-financial drivers could be our primary objective to do good in the world or might an incidental objective to minimise the harm we do as we succeed commercially. These financial and non-financial drivers may be in tension or in perfect harmony.

How worldly values feature in UK University strategies. University strategies talk about money a lot. 25 of the 36 strategies (69%) analysed for this book (Appendix 1) stress the strategic importance of financial sustainability (or financial stability or strong financial performance etc). Yet only five universities (14%) surface this financial commitment explicitly in their values (Aberdeen, Birmingham, LSE, Oxford Brookes and Plymouth).

Of all the core values cited by UK universities in their strategies, very few are about how they see their organisation's place in the world. This is odd because a lot of what is talked about in these strategies IS about their place in the world; its just that these aspirations don't find their way into university core values. Maybe they should, to a greater extent, in the future.

'Organisational' core values

Worldly core values
Organisational core values
People & Team core values

Organisational core values. What values could we come up with to reflect how we see ourselves as an organisation? These will be values related to our organisational identity. For most organisations there are two types of organisational drivers. Firstly, those demonstrating our conformance to the norms or standards of our type of organisation (how we, as an organisation, fit in) and secondly those demonstrating how we are distinctive from our peers or competitors (how we, as an organisation, stand out).

How organisational values feature in UK University strategies. In the university strategy research conducted for this book (Appendix 1), Warwick University's strategy says "… universities do not just follow fashion. They must stand for constant values and behaviours: for excellence, for the positive impact of their work on society, for rejecting intolerance and for both academic freedom and freedom of speech. Our strategy is underpinned by these values …" This both celebrates their 'university-ness' and clarifies which aspects of university-ness they identify with most.

St Mary's University, London introduces their values with this: "Rooted in our Catholic Foundation, with the value of the human person at its heart, our values set us apart, shape our behaviour and inform all our decisions in a university that responds to the demands of today." They clearly feel that values give rise to a key part of their distinctiveness, as a university.

These, however, are exceptions. In general, university strategies use statements of vision and mission to define both their university-ness and their distinctiveness. Their values seem surprisingly disconnected from vision and mission. Or perhaps more accurately, they do not make clear how their values will enable them to live their mission and pursue their vision.

'People & Team' core values

Worldly core values
Organisational core values
People & Team core values

People and Team core values. What values could we come up with to reflect how we would wish our people and teams to see themselves and conduct themselves within our organisation? Ideally these values should enable people and teams to see their role in the organisation as valued and purposeful, as principled and ethical, as consistent and reliable and as constructive and strategic.

How people and team values feature in UK University strategies. This is what the core values of university strategies are mostly about. Not all university strategies explain the purpose of their core values but, when they do, it is usually about guiding the decisions and actions of people and teams.

The University of Winchester says *"Our values [...] will guide and drive all our work, provide a decision-making and behavioural framework for staff, and outline the expectations that we have of our students and graduates."*

Middlesex University calls their core values 'community principles' and explains that they *"... guide how we work, learn and behave as a community. They are for everyone that makes up our global Middlesex family – staff, students and partners."*

The University of Greenwich introduce their values with this: *"Our shared values help us articulate and demonstrate to our community what we value. They guide us to adopt and embrace behaviours that will help us achieve our strategic plan and distinguish us from others. Our values also set clear expectations for our whole community about the behaviours that inform how we work and are recognised."*

The University of East Anglia state: *"Shaped by staff, our UEA values represent a core set of standards for how we behave as an employer, drive excellence in teaching, learning and research, and collaborate as an anchor institution in our local community. From tackling global challenges, striving for student and staff success, and creating a vibrant inclusive environment, our values are what unite us."*

Explicitly articulate core values

Large US Corporations

82%

of large corporations explicitly articulate core values

In a review of the websites and annual reports of 689 large, mostly US, corporations, Sull et al (2020) found that 562 (82%) explicitly articulated a set of core values. This is consistent with the review of the websites of the Standard & Poor's 500 companies by Guiso et al (2015) that found 85% had a section on corporate culture, citing values such as innovation, integrity and respect.

UK Universities

97%

of UK universities explicitly articulate core values

A review of the strategies of 36 UK universities sampled for this book (Appendix 1) revealed that 35 of them (97%) explicitly articulated core values. This is consistent with Barnett's (2022) suggestion that "the university is necessarily a value-laden institution" (p37).

How many core values?

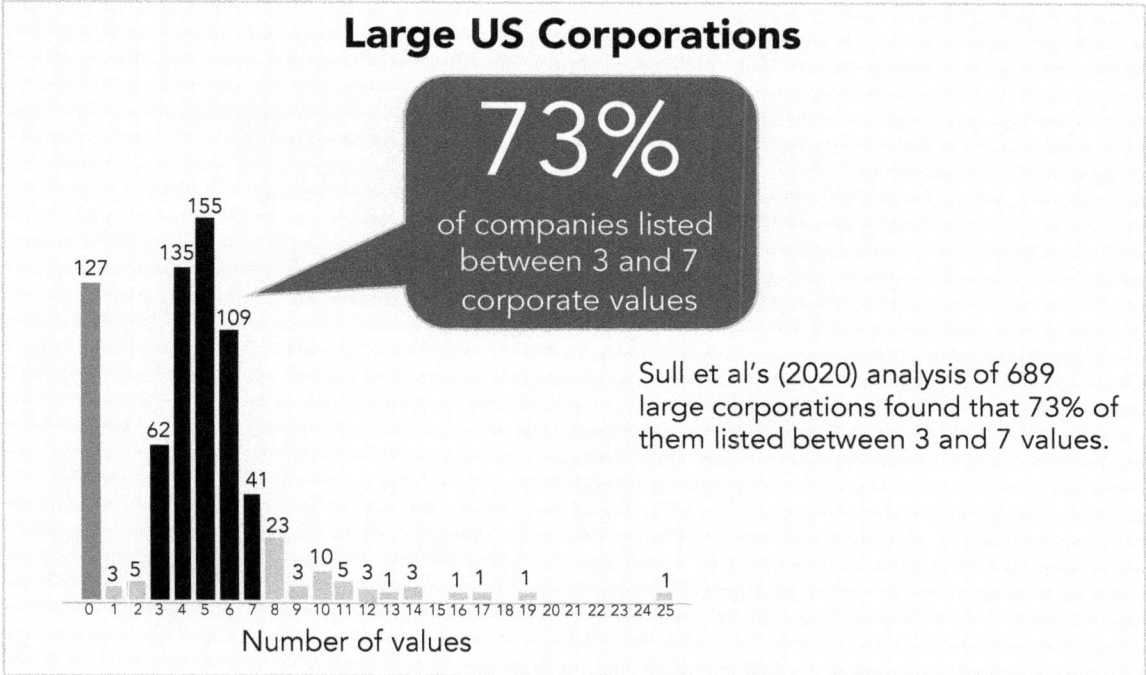

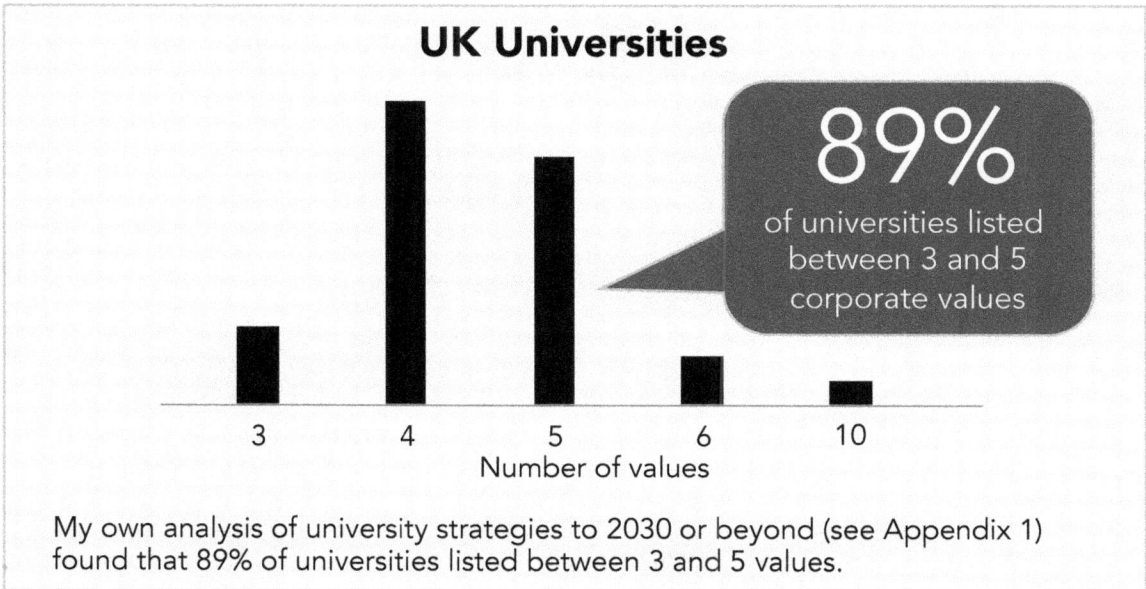

Large US Corporations

73%

of companies listed between 3 and 7 corporate values

Sull et al's (2020) analysis of 689 large corporations found that 73% of them listed between 3 and 7 values.

Number of values

UK Universities

89%

of universities listed between 3 and 5 corporate values

Number of values

My own analysis of university strategies to 2030 or beyond (see Appendix 1) found that 89% of universities listed between 3 and 5 values.

Most frequent core values

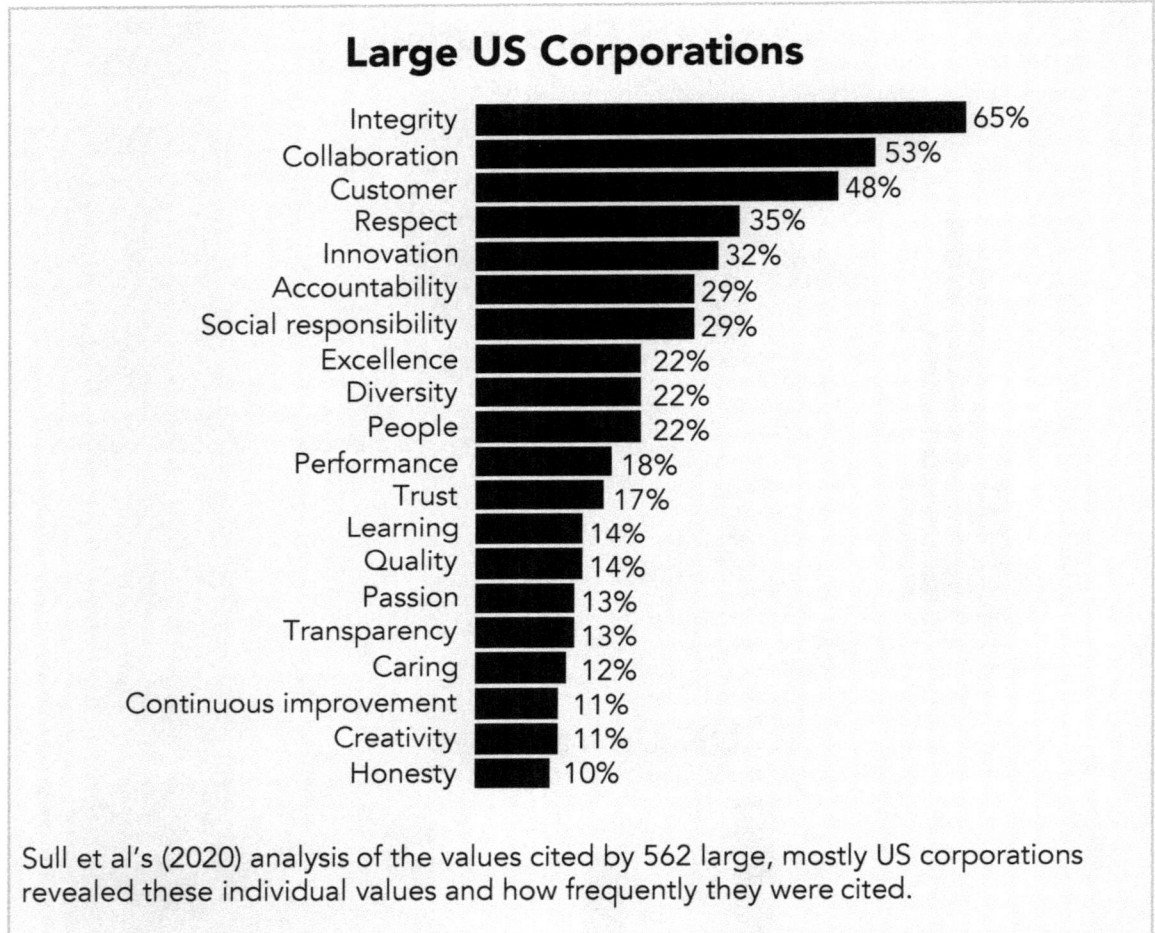

Large US Corporations

Value	Percentage
Integrity	65%
Collaboration	53%
Customer	48%
Respect	35%
Innovation	32%
Accountability	29%
Social responsibility	29%
Excellence	22%
Diversity	22%
People	22%
Performance	18%
Trust	17%
Learning	14%
Quality	14%
Passion	13%
Transparency	13%
Caring	12%
Continuous improvement	11%
Creativity	11%
Honesty	10%

Sull et al's (2020) analysis of the values cited by 562 large, mostly US corporations revealed these individual values and how frequently they were cited.

Core values are different in different sectors

Sull et al's (2020) data also suggest that core values appear to vary systematically between different industry sectors. 79% of IT Hardware companies cite 'innovation' as one of their values but only 7% cite 'diversity' as a value. By contrast, 45% of Regional Banks cite 'diversity' as a value but 0% of them cite 'innovation' as a value.

A full list the 62 corporate values cited by Sull et al (2020) is given in Appendix 2, along with the list of 68 values cited by UK universities in the research for this report.

Most frequent core values

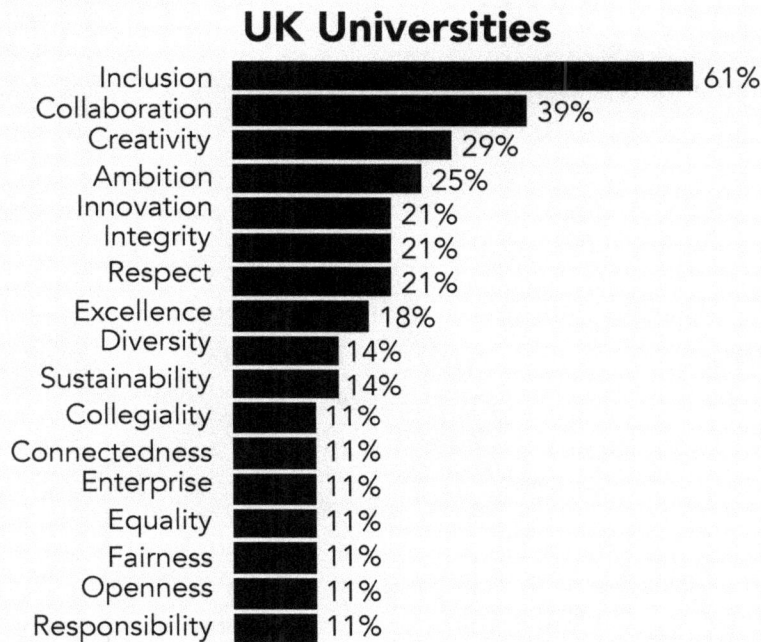

UK Universities

Value	Percentage
Inclusion	61%
Collaboration	39%
Creativity	29%
Ambition	25%
Innovation	21%
Integrity	21%
Respect	21%
Excellence	18%
Diversity	14%
Sustainability	14%
Collegiality	11%
Connectedness	11%
Enterprise	11%
Equality	11%
Fairness	11%
Openness	11%
Responsibility	11%

My own analysis (research conducted for this book - see Appendix 1) of the values labelled as such by 28 UK universities (of the 35 university strategies that cited values at all), revealed these individual values and how frequently they were cited.

Do core values change over time?

Comparing my earlier analysis (conducted Dec 2018 to Feb 2019) with my more recent analysis (Oct 2022 to Jan 2023) there are hints that university values may have changed over that period. Collaboration, for example, moved from earlier appearing in 20% of university strategies to now appearing in 39% of university strategies. Perhaps for similar reasons, the values 'equality' and 'connectedness' now feature in university strategies where they did not feature previously. Evidence of a change in values over time from larger data sets comes from a comparison of Sull et al (2020) with Guiso et al (2015).

	Research conducted	# companies	'Innovation' cited as a value
Guiso et al	2011	500	80%
Sull et al	2018	689	32%

Make core values matter

In the middle of our Core Values Framework on page 10 lies the challenge of how we make core values matter within organisations . We can do this by ensuring that they have their intended impact and that they are compelling in their presentation.

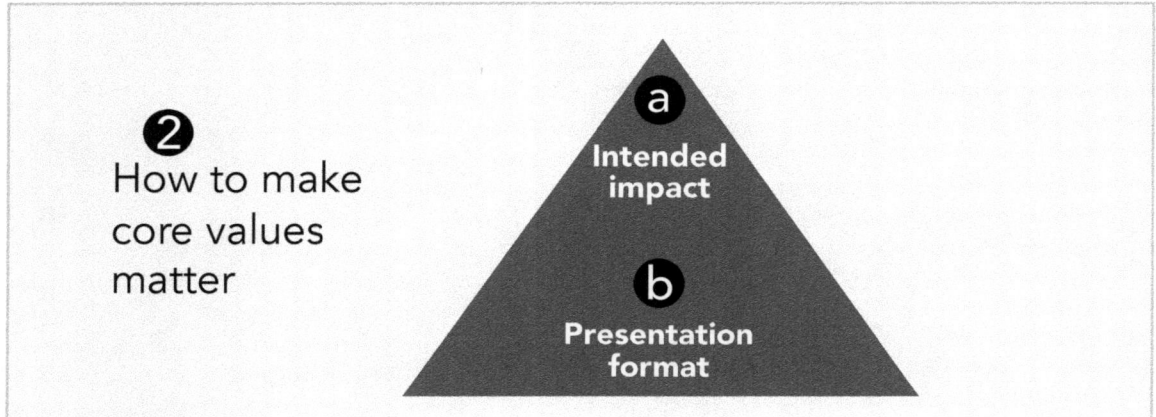

❷ How to make core values matter

a Intended impact

b Presentation format

We will begin our exploration of this challenge with research showing that merely stating values doesn't make them matter nor does it make them have any impact. We will then explore presentation formats for core values and question how well these presentation methods are likely to make core values matter within organisations.

Not all core values have their intended impact

Boeing had the core values of 'integrity, quality and safety' as it made the sequence of errors that led to two plane crashes, 346 deaths, the grounding of all 737 Max aircraft for 20 months and a financial settlement of $2.5B after being charged with fraudulently hiding information from security regulators.

Similarly, at the time of their collapse, U.S. energy, commodities and services company, Enron Corporation, had the published core values of 'respect, integrity, communication and excellence'. Following massive financial fraud, Enron filed for bankruptcy in 2001, leaving thousands of staff redundant and billions of dollars lost in shareholder funds and pensions.

Make core values matter: research

Our Core Values Framework suggests that, once we have chosen our core values, we then need to make sure they matter, that they will make a difference and make an impact on our organisation. Fortunately, there is some great research to get us started on this journey.

Sull et al (2020) set out to find out whether large US corporations 'walk the talk' when it comes to values. To do this they analysed what corporations declared their values to be (from websites and annual reports). Then they analysed what employees actually said about these same corporations in reviews on Glassdoor. Their conclusion? *"The analysis reveals that there is no correlation between the cultural values a company emphasizes in its published statements and how well the company lives up to those values in the eyes of employees."*

An earlier study by Guiso et al (2015), was more narrowly focused but took the story a step further. They looked at the value 'integrity' and, like Sull et al's study, compared its appearance in published value statements with employee reports of integrity in the Great Place to Work Institute's survey data. They discovered that financial performance correlated significantly with employee's actual experience of integrity but had no such correlation with the company's declaration of integrity in value statements.

The takeaway from this?

Merely declaring core values does very little on its own. It doesn't persuade people that they are real and its doesn't change their ways of working for the better. To make core values matter requires them to be clearly explained, self-evidently useful and readily applied to real-world decisions and actions.

Presentation formats for core values

Within their strategy documents, UK universities vary considerably in the detail with which they articulate their core values. Here is a range of presentation formats, ranging from single word labels to more descriptive statements.

Single word labels (examples from Queens University Belfast):
- Integrity
- Connectivity
- Ambition
- Respect
- Excellence

Paired values (examples from Staffordshire University):
- Ambitious and inspirational
- Fair and inclusive
- Curious and daring
- Innovative and enterprising

Themed values (examples from University College, London):
- Commitment to excellence and advancement on merit
- Fairness and equality
- Diversity
- Collegiality and community building
- Inclusiveness
- Openness
- Ethically acceptable standards of conduct
- Fostering innovation and creativity
- Developing leadership
- Environmental sustainability

Descriptive value statements (examples from University of Wolverhampton):
- Behave respectfully and ethically in all that we do
- Be inclusive and fair in our interactions with each other and with our wider community
- Act professionally, transparently, confidently, collaboratively and challengingly when engaging with our communities locally and globally
- Listen and learn from others

Presentation formats for core values

Finally, here is a much more **decision- and action-oriented articulation of core values**:

📝

INCLUSIVITY

We take positive steps to create an environment in which we celebrate, value, and provide equal opportunity to all.

EXEMPLAR BEHAVIOURS

- Critically examining your own biases and behaviours both through self-reflection and feedback from others

- Promptly addressing misunderstandings that may arise from your behaviour

- Listening with an open mind to understand different points of view

- Ensuring that your work / study is not overly influenced by a small number of contributors / perspectives

- When leading any activities being mindful, and taking proactive steps to ensure, that all participants have an opportunity to achieve their potential.

From Oxford Brookes University, in the r Strategy 2035

Presentation formats for core values

Taking a detailed approach to describing core values has been hailed as best-practice for commercial organisations (Sull et al, 2020). Here are three examples:

This is how one of Amazon's 'leadership principles', called 'Invent and Simplify', is described (Amazon, 2023):

> "Leaders expect and require innovation and invention from their teams and always find ways to simplify. They are externally aware, look for new ideas from everywhere, and are not limited by "not invented here." As we do new things, we accept that we may be misunderstood for long periods of time."

This is how Biogen describe their aspiration for all employees to be 'pioneering' (Biogen, 2023):

> "We challenge the status quo and experiment to create new possibilities. We take calculated risks and learn from failure. We are resilient and navigate through ambiguity with determination to innovate. We encourage candor to test assumptions and uncover the best ideas. We are open about what we do not know and ask questions to understand."

Tech recruiting platform talent.io have a core value called 'Think team' and this is how they turn it into action (Azoulay, 2017):

- Conflict happens - stay aware of that.
- It's not OK to be aggressive towards others, but it's OK to really defend your opinion if you feel strongly about it. Be hard on the problems, soft on the people.
- If a conflict arises, you should address it immediately and face to face.
- If you can't resolve it, it's OK to involve a mediator - another team member trusted by both parties.

Clarifying intended impact of core values

It is clear from the research of Sull et al (2020) and Guiso et al (2015) that core values need to be clearly explained, self-evidently useful and readily applied to real-world decisions and actions if they are going to be impactful. To do so, we need to opt for the more descriptive, decision- and action-oriented formats for presenting core values.

If, however, we are aiming for impactful core values, we need to be clear about what particular type of impact we seek. Obviously, if we are a commercial organisation, the ultimate impact we seek is probably increased revenue leading to greater profits. It is less obvious, however, how this impact might derive from organisational core values. We cannot simply 'believe' more profits into existence. So, when we talk of the impact of core values we are typically referring to a change in organisational culture that, in turn will lead to some greater good (e.g. commercial success or making the world a better place).

Some values translate readily into impact. If we have 'innovation' as a core value, we would expect 'a more innovative organisation' to be the resulting impact. Other values have a few more intermediate steps involved. If we have 'customer-focus' as a core value we would expect happier customers as a result and this may cascade on to more loyal customers who continue to be customers for longer periods. Yet other values have lengthy chains of consequences leading to meaningful impact. Having the value 'collaboration', for example, ought to make work across departments more effective and efficient. This, then could have many consequences. Big, digital transformation projects might progress more smoothly. Organisation re-designs might be less problematic. Agility in response to changing market conditions may be more rapid.

So, whilst core values could bring about culture change with lots of different beneficial impacts for the organisation, the challenge, as we devise these core values in the first place, is to determine what impact we would like to bring about and what feasibly do we believe we could bring about. We will return to this in the early stages of the Core Values Workflow in Part 3 of this book, as we scope out the intended purpose of core values.

What next, after core values?

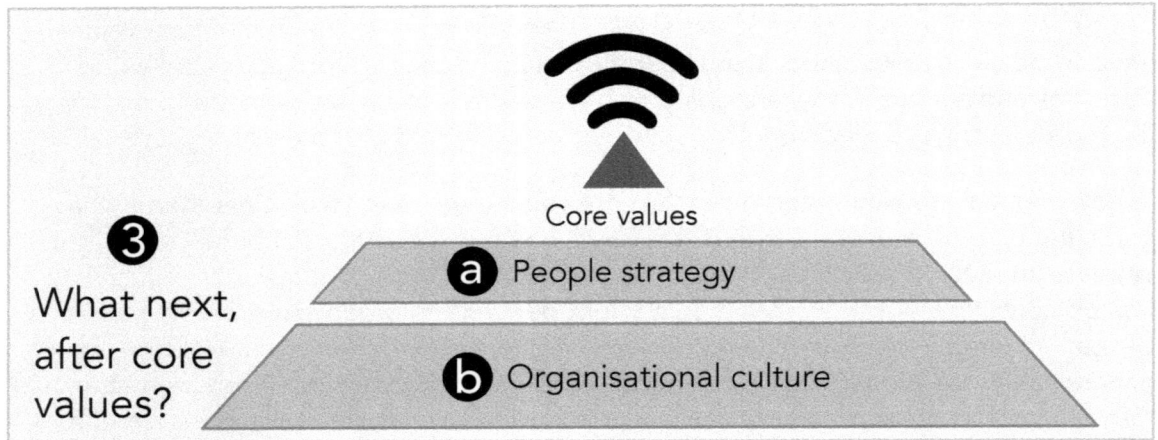

At the foot of our Core Values Framework lies the question 'What next, after core values?' The answer is that they will typically sit at the heart of a people strategy and help shape organisational culture.

How values and strategy fit together

Starting with strategy, we will explore how values and strategy fit together, using my House of Strategy Model (Baxter, 2020). We then need to take a step back and question what we mean when we talk of strategy in relation to core values. Are we talking about a people strategy or the people aspect of an overall organisational strategy. This begs the bigger question: should organisations have one strategy or many. Then we will explore some key principles for aligning core values and strategy.

Core values and organisational culture

To begin addressing organisational culture, we will set the scene with some quotes on its importance and the ten elements of culture that matter most to employees. Next, we will explore two dimensions of culture and how organisations can move across these dimensions. Then we explore our seven suggestions for changing organisational culture in general and, finally, consider how to align core values and culture.

Moving from core values to strategy and to organisational culture is a big topic and it will inevitably need a lot of fine tuning to make it work for your organisation. But these tools ought to make your thinking and your work on core values a lot more structured, a lot more deliberate and hopefully a lot more impactful than it would have been without them.

People strategy & culture: the basics

People Strategy – Defined

A people strategy is an organisation's approach to attracting, developing and retaining people & teams in order to achieve strategic success. It sets out a deliberate approach to managing relations between people across the entire organisation and at all stages of the employee lifecycle.

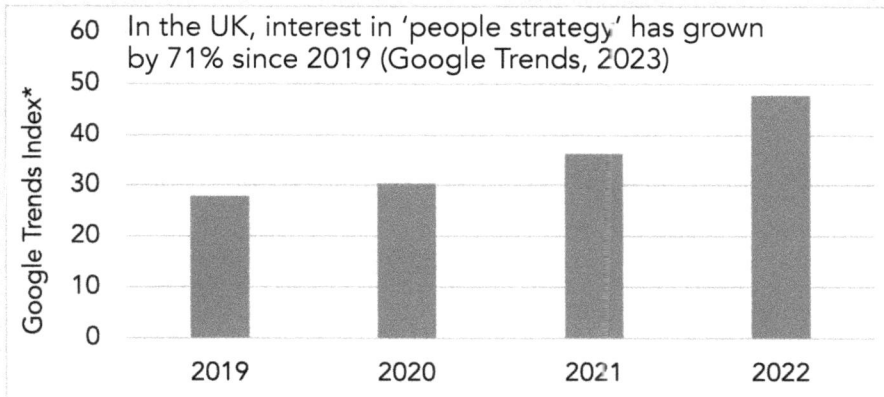

In the UK, interest in 'people strategy' has grown by 71% since 2019 (Google Trends, 2023)

Google Trends Index* — bar chart showing values for:
- 2019: ~27
- 2020: ~30
- 2021: ~36
- 2022: ~47

(Y-axis: 0, 10, 20, 30, 40, 50, 60)

*Google Trends reports the relative frequency of searches over time on a normalised 0 to 100 scale

Organisational Culture - Defined

Organisational culture is the set of collective or shared values, beliefs, expectations, norms and practices which influence the behaviour of people as members of an organisation. It influences the way people interact, how individuals and groups learn, and how they embrace or resist change.

The importance of organisational culture

Building a strong culture provides consistency and direction, guides decisions and actions and fuels the workforce to reach their full potential. It is the 'glue' that aligns and integrates everyone across the organisation, towards a shared purpose. It encourages empathy and collaboration, creating a sense of community and cohesion. It helps people feel their voice matters and is being heard. It makes individuals feel valued by the organisation and, in turn, helps them to feel that the organisation deserves to be valued by them.

House of Strategy Model

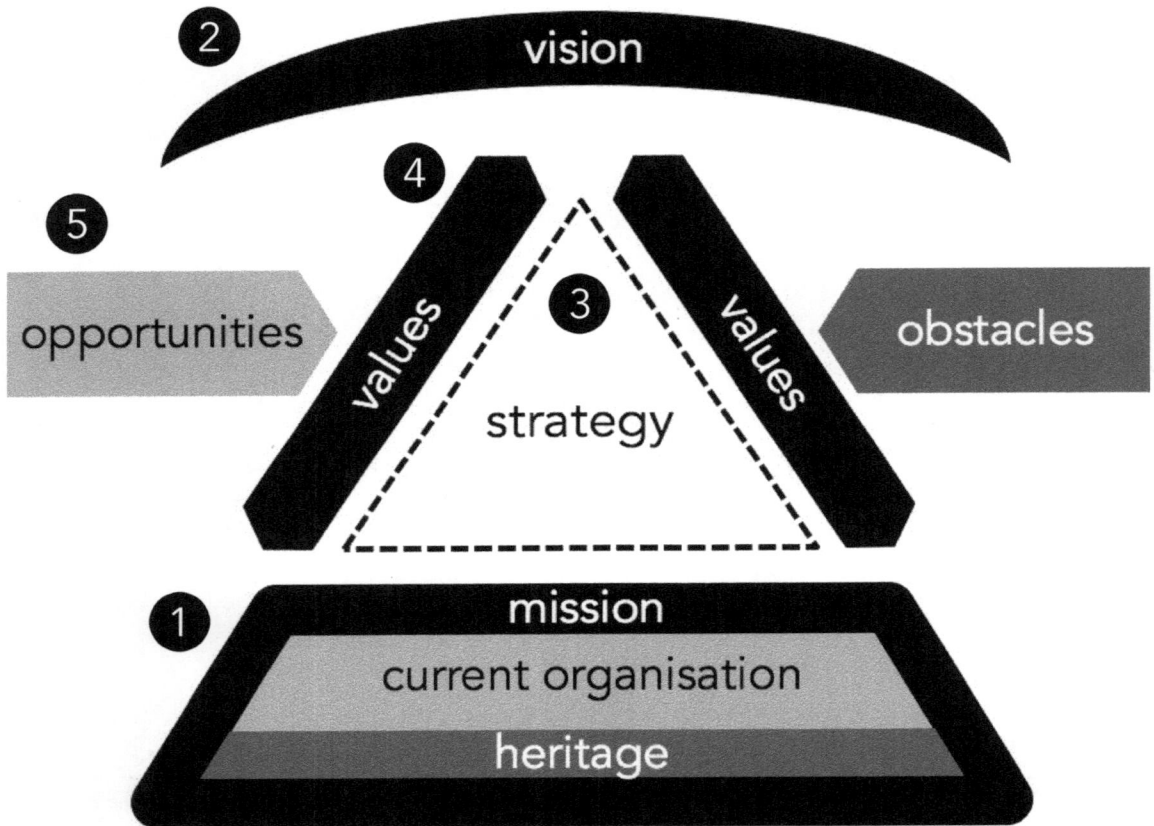

Values are like guard-rails, guiding the acceptable ways in which we strive to achieve strategic success

(Model available at goalatlas.com/house-of-strategy/)

How values and strategy fit together

My House of Strategy Model (Baxter, 2020) sets out how vision, mission, values and strategy fit together in a structured and systematic way.

1 Your current organisation is the baseline for any strategy. For all but the freshest of start-ups, your organisation's current state will be derived from its heritage; how the organisation originated and what capabilities it has since acquired. Current state ought to be characterised, to a large extent, by 'mission'. An organisation's mission is a statement of core purpose and focus, that normally remains unchanged over time. It answers the question, "Why does our business exist?" A mission statement communicates the organisation's purpose to its employees, customers, suppliers and other stakeholders and creates a sense of identity for its employees.

2 An organisation's vision is almost a counter-point to its current state. It defines where we want to be, in contrast to where we are currently. An organisation's vision is a picture of its potential, an audacious dream of its future. It should inform, inspire and energise everyone in the organisation. Since vision typically stretches into the future, it is also what gives continuity from one strategy to the next.

3 Strategy is how we move from where we are now to where we want to be by defining the future state we seek to bring about. It is what connects current state (mission) with a picture of our potential (vision).

4 Strategy is driven by, and constrained by, the organisation's values. The word 'values' literally means principles or standards of behaviour; one's judgement of what is important in life; the moral principles and beliefs or accepted standards of a person or social group. Values are the ethical ideals of the organisation. They are important and lasting beliefs or ideals shared by the members of a culture about what is good or bad and desirable or undesirable.

5 Strategy is also driven by and constrained by the opportunities and obstacles presented by the organisation's operating environment. These can include changing customer needs, emerging technologies and new laws or regulations.

One strategy ... or many?

As we saw earlier, there has been a rise in interest in the concept of 'people strategy', as indicated by Google searches for the phrase. This, then begs the question what exactly do we mean by a people strategy. Is it separate thing from an overarching corporate or organisation-wide strategy? Many organisations claim to have multiple strategies. Here are some examples from my analysis of UK university strategies:

- The University of Leeds strategy links to four other strategies: 1. Research and Innovation Strategy, 2. Student Education Strategy, 3. Digital Transformation Strategy and 4. International Strategy.

- Manchester Metropolitan University explain that they "have developed enabling strategies to help us realise our 2030 ambition, including investment in our people, campus and technology, commitment to sustainability, inclusion and our local communities, and ensuring we retain strong financial foundations."

- The University of Suffolk have five supporting strategies: 1. Learning, Teaching and Assessment, 2. Research and Scholarly Activity, 3. Business Engagement, 4. International and 5. People and Places.

- The University of the West of England lists seven supporting strategies: 1. Teaching and Learning, 2. Research, 3. Community and Business Engagement, 4. Climate Action and Sustainability, 5. Equality, Diversity and Inclusivity, 6. Health and Wellbeing and 7. People.

Having seen strategies being deployed in many different ways in many different organisations, my conclusion is that it is perfectly fine to have many different strategy documents, serving the interests of different groups of people across the organisation. All these documents, however, need to have such coherence that it is probably best to think of them as facets of a single underlying strategy. This could be thought of as a 'one strategy, many strategy documents' approach. This approach could be visualised on a strategy map as follows:

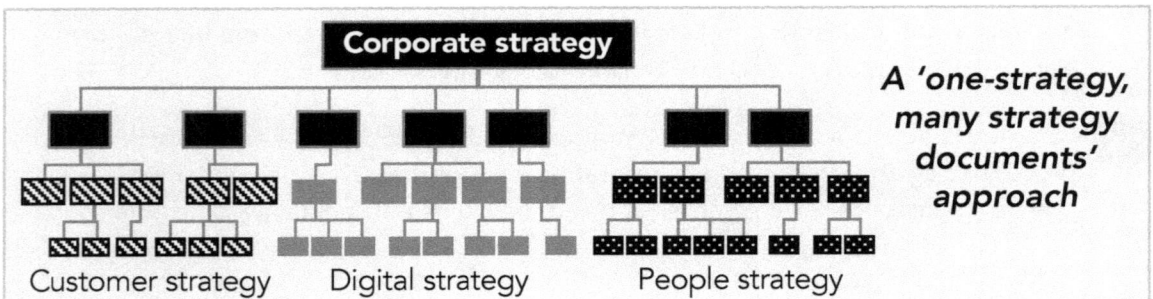

Corporate strategy

A 'one-strategy, many strategy documents' approach

Customer strategy   Digital strategy   People strategy

Aligning core values & strategy

By deciding upon core values, we have already made some big strategic decisions

When we were thinking about which core values might be the right ones for us, we distinguished between values with different drivers.

Worldly
Organisational
People & Team

Are our values going to be about **worldly issues**: market positioning ('leading innovator in our sector') or environmental sustainability ('leave a healthy planet for our children')?

Or **organisational issues**: how will we fit in with other similar organisations ('as a university we will celebrate & uphold academic freedom') of how will we stand out in our sector ('obsessively customer-focused')?

Or **people & team issues**: how we will maintain consistency ('continue to ensure a healthy and happy work-life balance for everyone") or how we will drive change ('take calculated risks and learn from failure')?

These are BIG strategic decisions. So big, in fact, that we cannot make them about core values in isolation; we need to cross-reference them with strategy. Similarly, if we have made some strategic decisions we need to cross reference them with core values. Ultimately, we need to strive for deep and impactful alignment between core values and strategy.

Three takeaways from this:

1. It is a lot easier to develop core values and strategy in parallel, rather than having one already finalised and having to retro-fit the other so it aligns.

2. This is inevitably an iterative process. Core values and strategy need to be repeatedly re-drafted and refined until they work in synergy – each informs and support the other.

3. Don't skimp on the effort here. It can take a LOT OF EFFORT to get the two to really fly together. But when they do the result can be just … beautiful!

Core values and organisational culture

"When we look at companies' web pages, we find that 85% of the Standard and Poor's 500 (S&P 500) companies have a section (sometimes even two) dedicated to - what they call - "corporate culture," i.e. principles and values that should inform the behavior of all the firms' employees."

from Guiso et al (2015, p61)

"Senior leaders ... love to talk about their company culture. Over the past three decades, more than three-quarters of CEOs interviewed in a major business magazine discussed their company's culture or core values - even when not specifically asked about it.

Organisations and employees both talk about values as the foundation of their organisational culture."

from Sull et al (2020)

Core values and organisational culture

"Our culture is based on our shared values"

University of Birmingham (2021)

"Culture is the living of your values"

Jeff Lawson (2015)

" ... poorly implemented values can poison a company's culture."

Patrick Lencioni (2002)

"Your goals are a definition of where you want to be and your values are a definition of the behaviours and attitudes that will help you to get there. Bringing goals and values together helps employees understand what is required of them and why."

James Allen (2022)

10 elements of culture that matter most to employees

1. **Employees feel respected** Employees are treated with consideration, courtesy, and dignity, and their perspectives are taken seriously.

2. **Leaders are supportive** Leaders help employees do their work, respond to requests, accommodate employees' individual needs, offer encouragement, and 'have their backs'.

3. **Leaders live core values** Leaders' actions are consistent with the organisation's values.

4. **Leaders avoid toxicity** Leaders must ensure their attitudes and actions never create a poisonous work environment.

5. **We all behave ethically** Managers and employees must always seek to act with integrity and guard against unethical behaviour.

6. **Fair benefits** Employees need to believe in the fairness of all employer-provided benefits.

7. **Reasonable amenities and perks** Employees should consider workplace amenities and perks to be reasonable and proportionate to the demands of the job.

8. **Meaningful learning and development** Employees should feel their opportunities for learning and development are meaningful to them personally and relevant to the work performance expected of them.

9. **Job security** Perceived job security, addressing fear of layoffs, offshoring, and automation.

10. **Reorganisations** Reorganisations are always disruptive. They shouldn't happen too frequently, nor too infrequently and should always be clearly justified.

Adapted from Sull & Sull (2021)

Dimension #1 of organisational culture

To see how core values can be used to influence culture, let's explore two dimensions of culture and how organisations can move across these dimensions.

Emergent   Deliberate

←———————————————————————————————————→

culture   culture

Emergent culture

Culture will tend to emerge without any intention on the part of leadership. Edgar Schein from MIT Sloan (Schein, 1990) first suggested that organisational culture is:

a) a pattern of basic assumptions,
(b) invented, discovered, or developed by a given group,
(c) as it learns to cope with its problems of external adaptation and internal integration,
(d) that has worked well enough to be considered valid and, therefore
(e) is to be taught to new members as the
(f) correct way to perceive, think, and feel in relation to those problems.

He went on to suggest that "the strength and degree of internal consistency of a culture are, therefore, a function of the stability of the group, the length of time the group has existed, the intensity of the group's experiences of learning, the mechanisms by which the learning has taken place (i.e., positive reinforcement or avoidance conditioning), and the strength and clarity of the assumptions held by the founders and leaders of the group."

Deliberate culture

Changing culture through the actions of leadership is difficult. Research suggests that efforts to change organisation culture succeed between 10% and 30% of the time (Smith, 2003). When it works, however, it can have huge impact. As Yves Pigneur points out "The right culture can change the art of what's possible in organizations." (Pigneur, 2017).

The secret, then, is not to seek to either destroy or create organisational culture but rather to align it with strategy. Change is achieved by nudging existing cultural norms and habits rather than by issuing demands or commands.

Consequently, a lot of what we will work through in the workflow section of this book will be about surfacing the core values that are already embedded in organisational culture and then either guiding them into strategy alignment or supplementing them with new values that we work to instil over time.

Dimension #2 of organisational culture

Cultural
aspiration

↑

Cultural aspiration

A culture that is aspirational is a set of positive, purpose-affirming, productive ideas, customs, and social behaviour, held widely across and organisation. More simply, the cultural aspiration of your organisation is who you aspire to be, collectively.

"... organizations that align on a clear aspiration across both performance and culture increase the odds of their transformation's success by 300 percent."

Daschle et al (2019)

Cultural despair

Introduced by Fritz Stern in 1961, cultural despair is characterised by a deep sense of collective unhappiness and helplessness. This helplessness is triggered by loss of control (or a perceived loss of control) and leads to apathy and resignation to acceptance of current circumstances, despite their unpleasantness.

It has been described as a "poisoned solidarity" - the communal intoxication forged from the negative energies of fear, suspicion and envy.

Hedges (2020)

↓

Cultural
despair

Combining the two dimensions of organisational culture

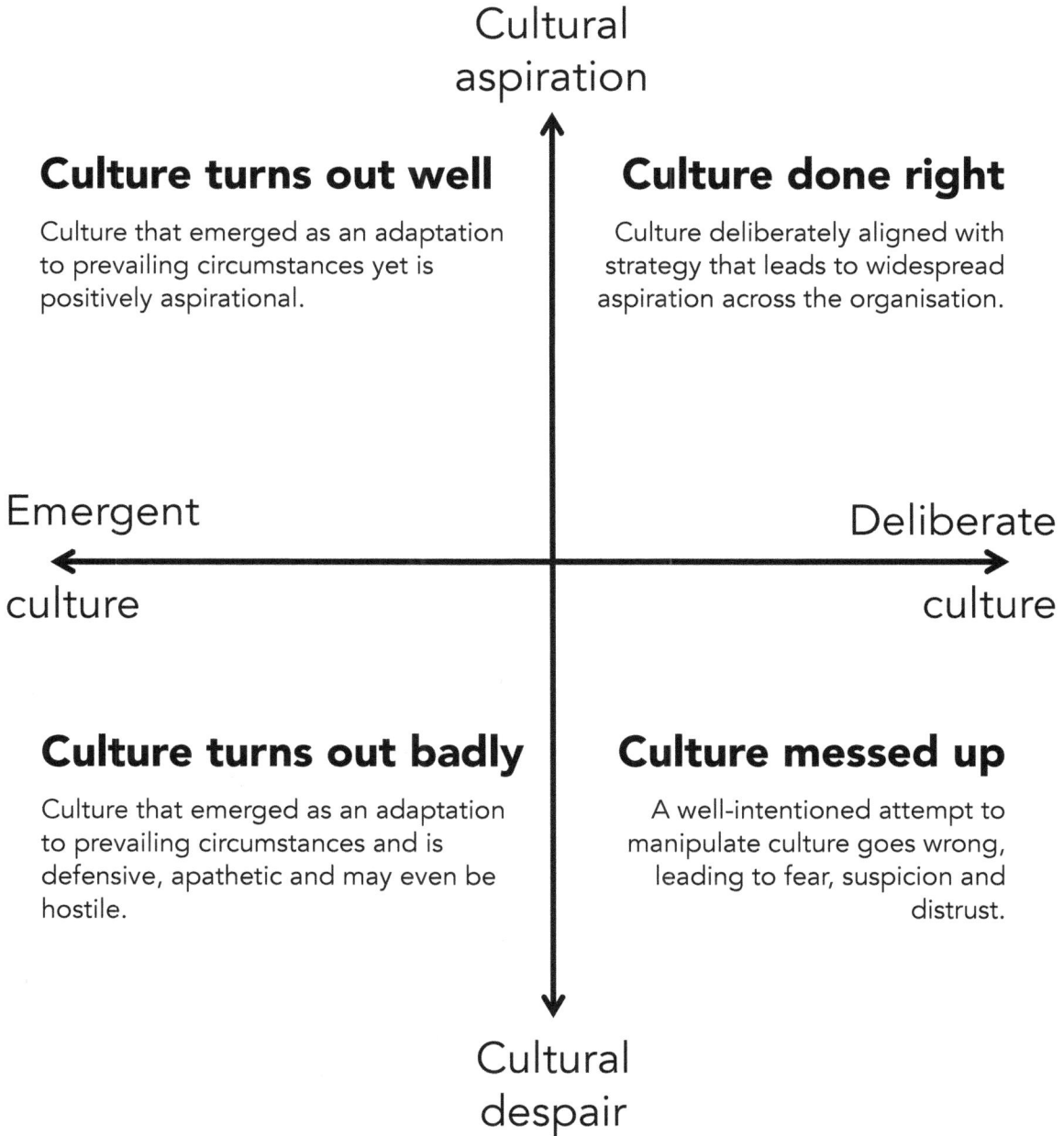

Cultural
aspiration

Culture turns out well

Culture that emerged as an adaptation to prevailing circumstances yet is positively aspirational.

Culture done right

Culture deliberately aligned with strategy that leads to widespread aspiration across the organisation.

Emergent

culture

Deliberate

culture

Culture turns out badly

Culture that emerged as an adaptation to prevailing circumstances and is defensive, apathetic and may even be hostile.

Culture messed up

A well-intentioned attempt to manipulate culture goes wrong, leading to fear, suspicion and distrust.

Cultural
despair

Two currents in organisational culture

There are two ways the cultural currents tend to flow within organisations. One is positive, for the health of the organisation and the wellbeing of its people, the other is negative.

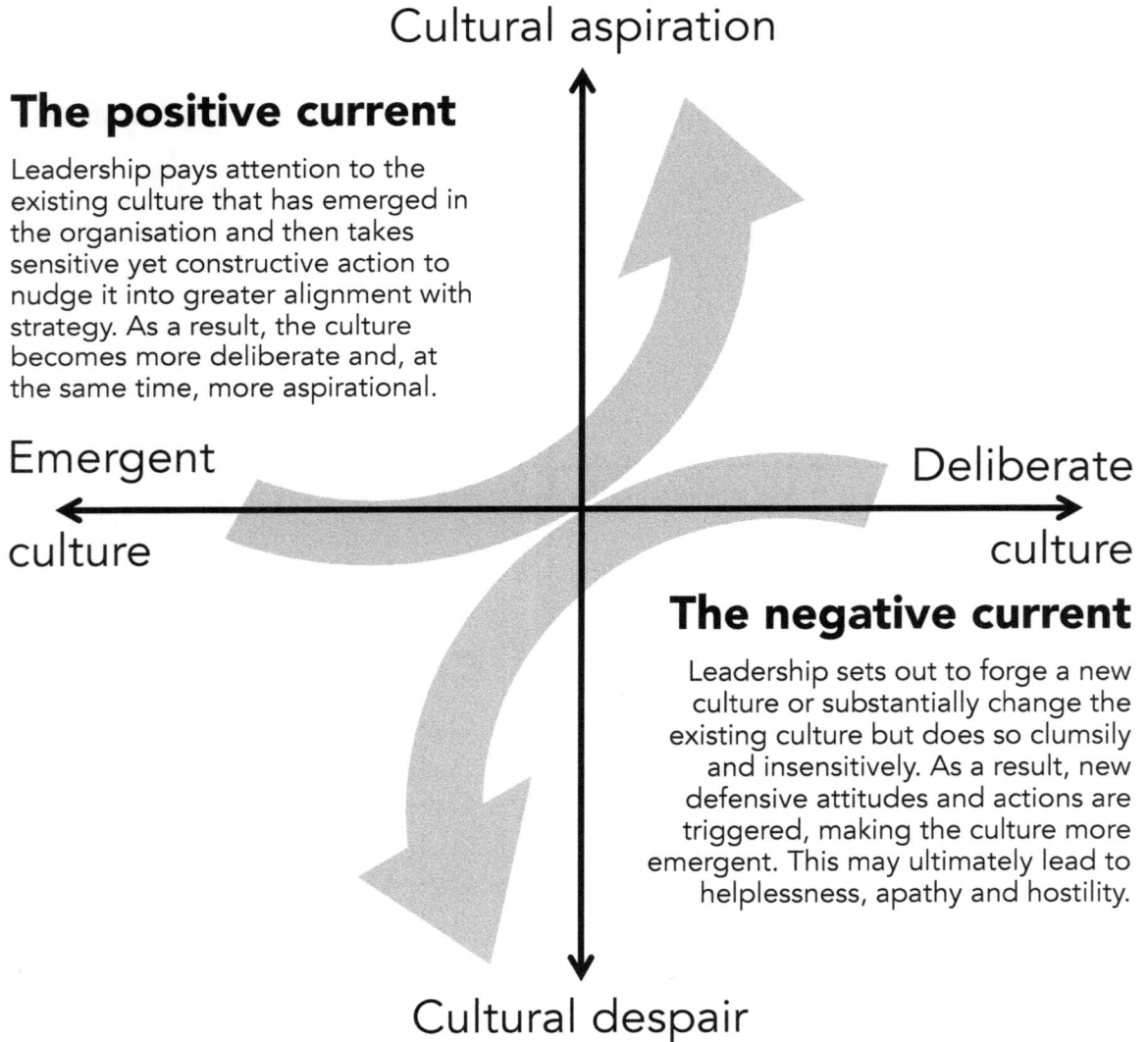

Cultural aspiration

The positive current

Leadership pays attention to the existing culture that has emerged in the organisation and then takes sensitive yet constructive action to nudge it into greater alignment with strategy. As a result, the culture becomes more deliberate and, at the same time, more aspirational.

Emergent
culture

Deliberate
culture

The negative current

Leadership sets out to forge a new culture or substantially change the existing culture but does so clumsily and insensitively. As a result, new defensive attitudes and actions are triggered, making the culture more emergent. This may ultimately lead to helplessness, apathy and hostility.

Cultural despair

Changing organisational culture

Here are seven suggestions for positive change:

1. Respect the emergent culture that already exists within the organisation.

2. Don't try to eliminate it or replace it. Instead nudge it into greater alignment.

3. When it comes to culture change, show don't tell - let people see the change in you rather than telling them what change you want to see in them.

4. Lead from the top towards cultural aspiration and encourage others to follow.

5. Recognise, reward and celebrate positive culture change.

6. Watch out for signs of negative cultural traits and invest in addressing the underlying issues.

7. Seek out flywheels of positive cultural change: curiosity leads to trying new things, leads to small wins, leads to awareness, leads to more curiosity.

Aligning core values & culture

Aligning core values with culture is a multi-factorial challenge: each core value is likely to influence multiple facets of organisational culture. To map and manage this relationship we use petal-scoring.

Petal-scoring core values and culture

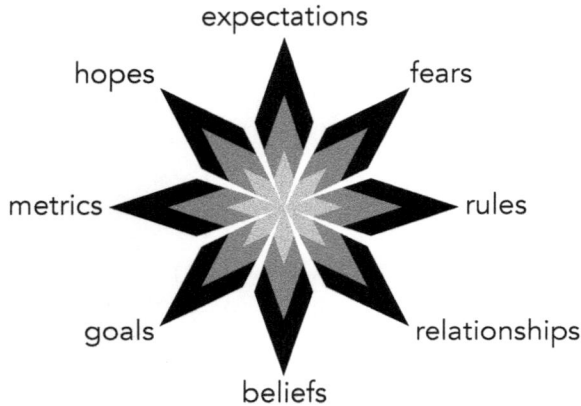

- Each petal represents one aspect of culture you could change (fears, rules etc.)
- For each core value, score which of these aspects of culture you think it will change and by how much:

little impact
moderate impact
big impact

Core value: Take calculated risks & learn from failure

Explaining the score: The main effect this core value will have on our culture is that it will enable us to set meaningful goals for innovation projects. Previously, many people felt they had to conceal their hopes for genuine experimentation due to fears of experiments failing to produce positive outcomes. Secondary effects ought to be much better relationships between experimenters and their line managers: both can be more open and honest about the risks and potential outcomes of experiments.

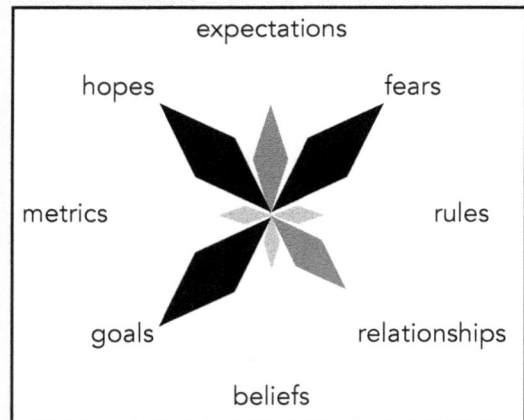

What else needs to change: Introduce a review process to check that our calculated risks are worth trying – they have the right risk / reward ratio. We also need to introduce post-project reviews to make sure we learn from our failures.

Words of wisdom on people strategy & organisational culture

"Manage the top line: your strategy, your people and your products, and the bottom line will follow."

Steve Jobs,
Founder
Apple

"The reason most people never reach their goals is that they don't define them, or ever seriously consider them as believable or achievable. Winners can tell you where they are going, what they plan to do along the way, and who will be sharing the adventure with them"

Cecil B DeMille
Film Director

"HR can become a strategic asset because the ability to execute well is a source of competitive advantage and people are the lynchpin of strategy execution"

Brian Becker,
Professor
University at Buffalo

"Customers will never love a company until the employees love it first."

Simon Sinek,
Author of
Start with Why

"An organization's ability to learn, and translate that learning into action rapidly, is the ultimate competitive advantage."

Jack Welch,
Chairman & CEO
General Electric

"Our culture is friendly and intense, but if push comes to shove we'll settle for intense"

Jeff Bezos,
Founder
Amazon

Part 3 The Core Values Workflow

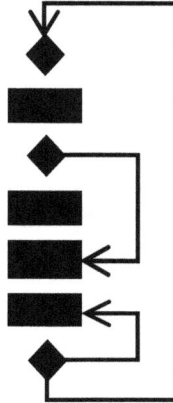

Scope core values

Devise / revise core values

Articulate & apply core values

Track & refine core values

Core Values Workflow

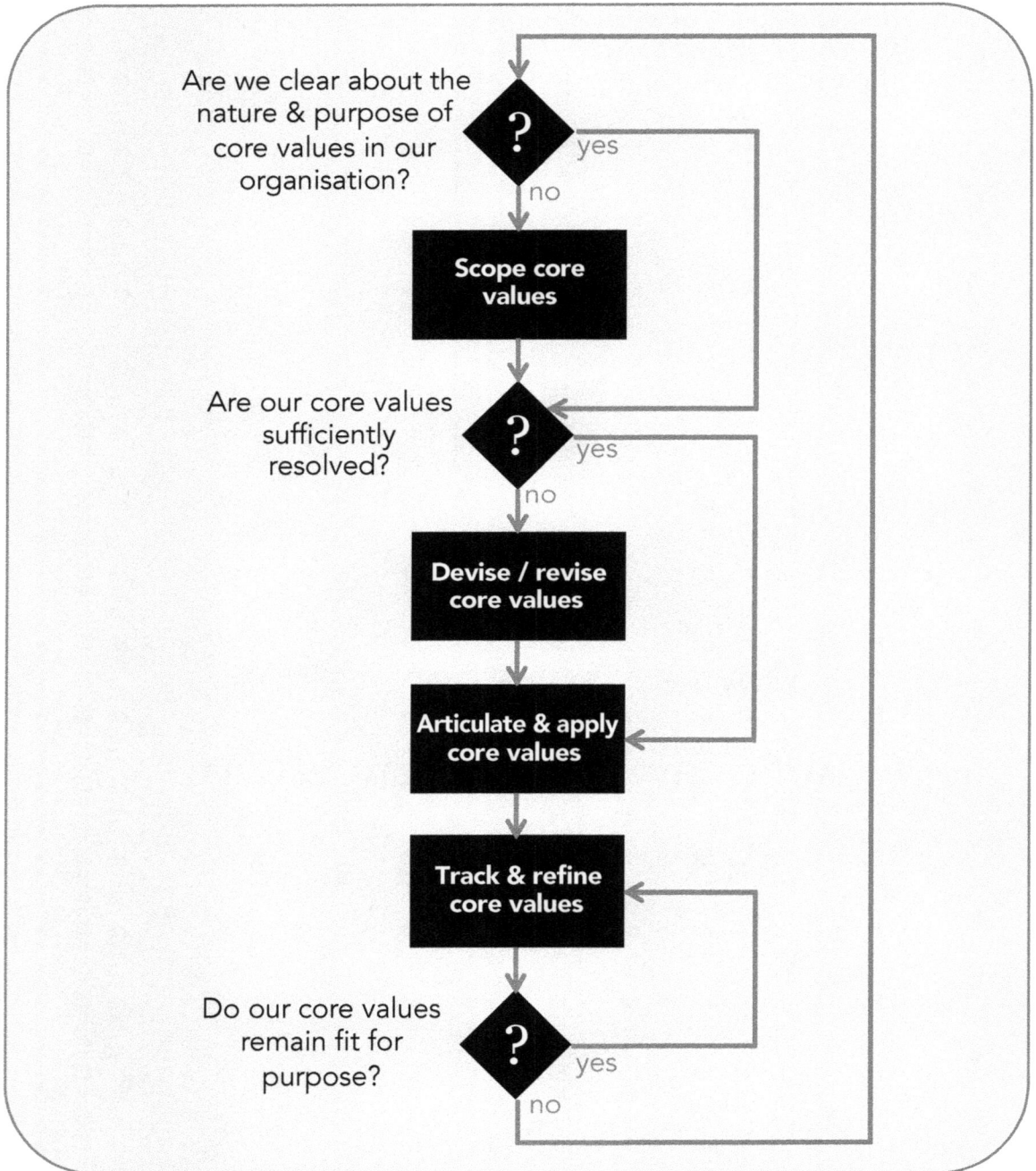

Are we clear about the nature & purpose of core values in our organisation?

?

yes

no

Scope core values

Are our core values sufficiently resolved?

?

yes

no

Devise / revise core values

Articulate & apply core values

Track & refine core values

Do our core values remain fit for purpose?

?

yes

no

Core Values Workflow

The Core Values Workflow can be used to devise, communicate and refine your organisation's core values.

The way this workflow is presented suggests a tidy linear process. This, of course, is a simplification to highlight the key elements and their primary relationships. In reality, this workflow is much more like an iterative design process. Core values will be tentatively chosen, only to find it is difficult to make them purposeful in any focused way. So new core values are chosen but they prove hard to articulate meaningfully. Loops are repeated within this workflow until a set of core values are settled upon which tick all the following boxes. They need to be:

☑ Readily articulated;

☑ Simple to grasp;

☑ Straightforward to apply;

☑ Meaningful for individuals;

☑ Purposeful for the organisation;

☑ Practical for tracking.

This is probably a more realistic representation of the workflow for producing and managing core values

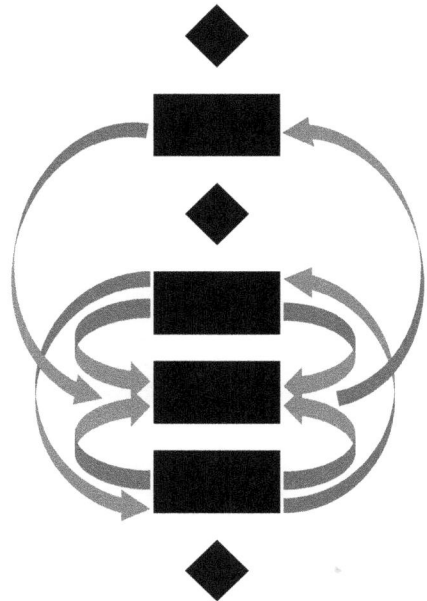

Core Values Workflow in more detail

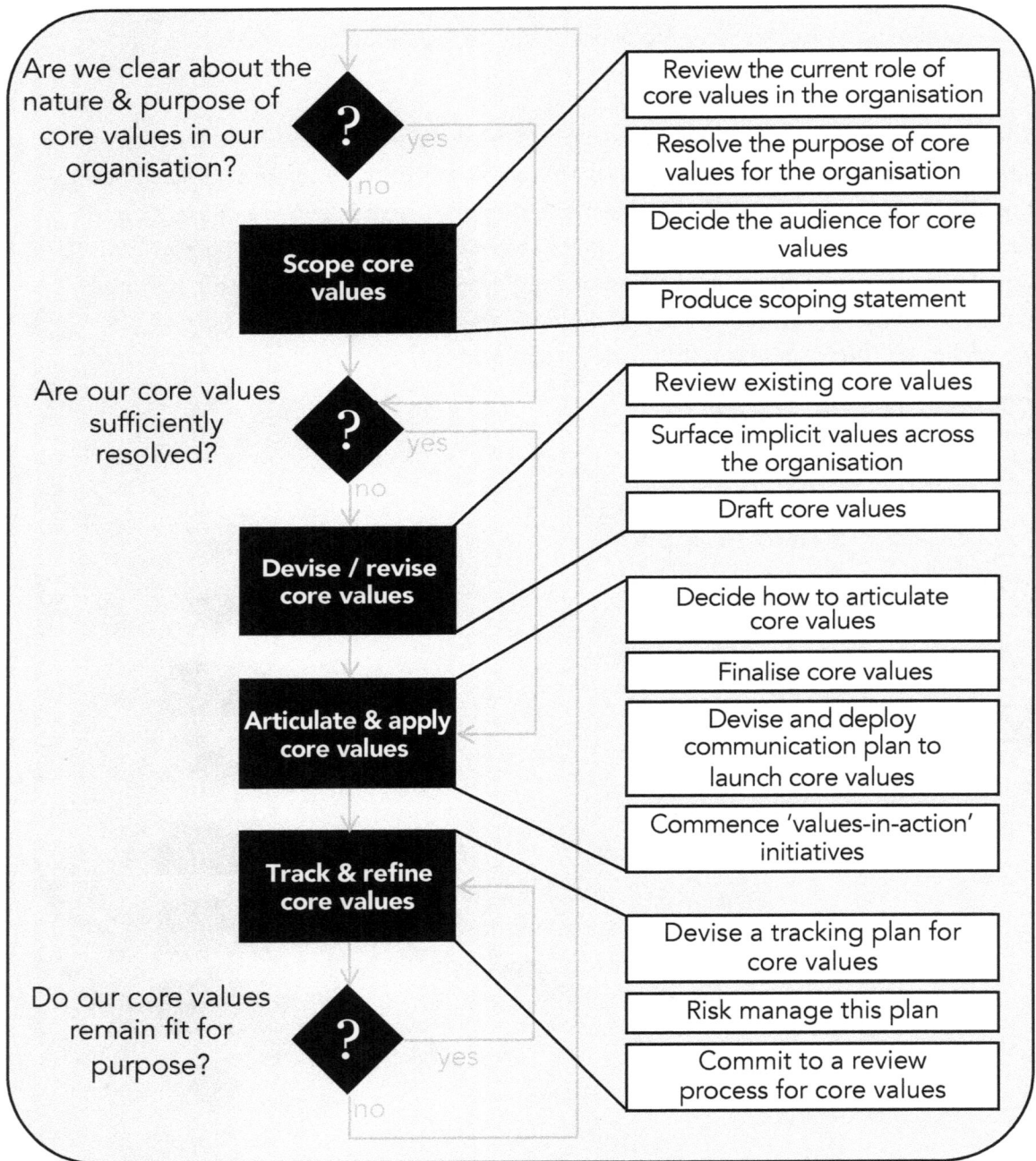

Are we clear about the nature & purpose of core values in our organisation?

? yes / no

Scope core values

- Review the current role of core values in the organisation
- Resolve the purpose of core values for the organisation
- Decide the audience for core values
- Produce scoping statement

Are our core values sufficiently resolved?

? yes / no

Devise / revise core values

- Review existing core values
- Surface implicit values across the organisation
- Draft core values

Articulate & apply core values

- Decide how to articulate core values
- Finalise core values
- Devise and deploy communication plan to launch core values
- Commence 'values-in-action' initiatives

Track & refine core values

Do our core values remain fit for purpose?

? yes / no

- Devise a tracking plan for core values
- Risk manage this plan
- Commit to a review process for core values

Scope core values

Here is the process for scoping core values. We will walk through each step in the process over the next few pages:

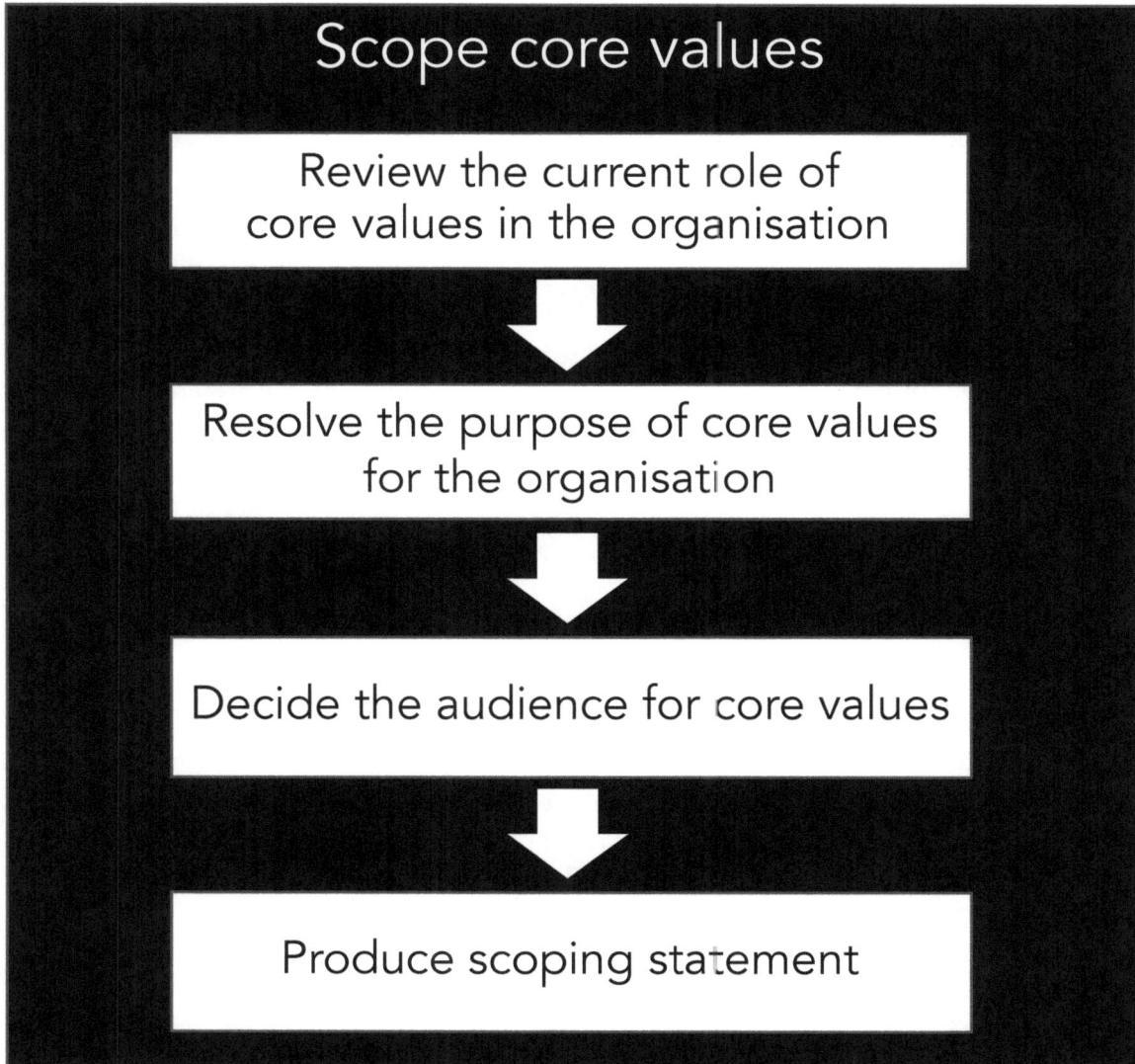

Scope core values

Review the current role of
core values in the organisation

⬇

Resolve the purpose of core values
for the organisation

⬇

Decide the audience for core values

⬇

Produce scoping statement

Scoping core values: the basics

What is 'scoping'?

To scope something is to determine its extent, its range or its boundaries and this often involves determining its focus, its essence or its nature.

What does it mean to 'scope' core values?

Scoping core values, therefore, determines what core values mean for an organisation and what they are going to be used for. It clarifies how an organisation's core values can be fit-for-purpose. Our Core Values Framework (described in Part 2) shows how core values can mean very different things to different organisations. This scoping process is designed to provoke conversation and debate about what core values ought to mean for our organisation. Are they, for example, a way to uphold tradition, or a manifesto for change? Resolving this debate means deciding what you want core values to mean for your own organisation; deciding in broad terms what purpose core values ought to serve, without prescribing the values themselves in any detail. You may even scope them by exclusion – this is what core values are *not* going to be.

What does the scoping process produce?

The decisions made during the scoping of core values are usually captured in a 'scoping statement'. For larger organisations, with more elaborate decision-making processes, the entire scoping process may need to be documented. This scoping statement or scoping document then acts as a reference for all further work on core values, checking that they remain fit for their intended purpose.

Review the current role of core values in the organisation

Scoping core values – step #1

'We have several versions of our core values in different documents and web pages'

'We have statements that look like core values, but we don't call them that'

'We have a single definitive set of core values'

'Nobody knows when our core values were written, nor who wrote them'

'Our core values have been reviewed and revised recently'

'We have no way of getting feedback from anyone about core values'

'We occasionally get hints on how people feel about values but it is hard to interpret and harder to act upon'

'Our annual staff survey asks specifically about our core values'

Range of possible outcomes

'We have no explicit core values'

'We do have explicit core values but they need to be completely re-written'

'Our core values need to be re-written whilst preserving some parts'

'We have good core values which may need minor editing'

It may be useful to include more qualitative information about the role of core values in the organisation. For example, 'our current core values are meaningless – nobody cares about them'; 'we have strong values but they are not articulated'; 'I'd love us to have an agreed set of core values – it would mean a lot to me'.

Resolve the purpose of core values for the organisation

Scoping core values – step #2

We need to be clear about what we want to achieve by having core values.

Here is how some UK universities described (or hinted at) the purpose of their core values:

- "[Our values] are our cultural cornerstones, guiding our decision-making and how we work together as a University community." **Bangor University**

- "Our culture is based on our shared values, which we seek to embody throughout the organisation." **University of Birmingham**

- "Our values are critical to providing a sense of identity and in helping to communicate our mission, vision and strategy across the Coventry University Group. They inform our practice and decision making and are essential for addressing challenges and opportunities." **Coventry University**

- "[Our] values represent a core set of standards for how we behave as an employer, drive excellence in teaching, learning and research, and collaborate as an anchor institution in our local community." **University of East Anglia**

- "Our shared values help us articulate and demonstrate to our community what we value. They guide us to adopt and embrace the behaviours that will help us achieve our strategic plan and distinguish us from others. Our values also set clear expectations for our whole university community about the behaviours that inform how we work and are recognised." **University of Greenwich**

Example: the purpose of Twilio's core values

Jeff Lawson, CEO and co-founder of Twilio, the communications technology platform, explained that their core values needed to address people, product and process issues across the organisation (adapted from Lawson, 2015).

Who you hire / fire and how
you treat one another

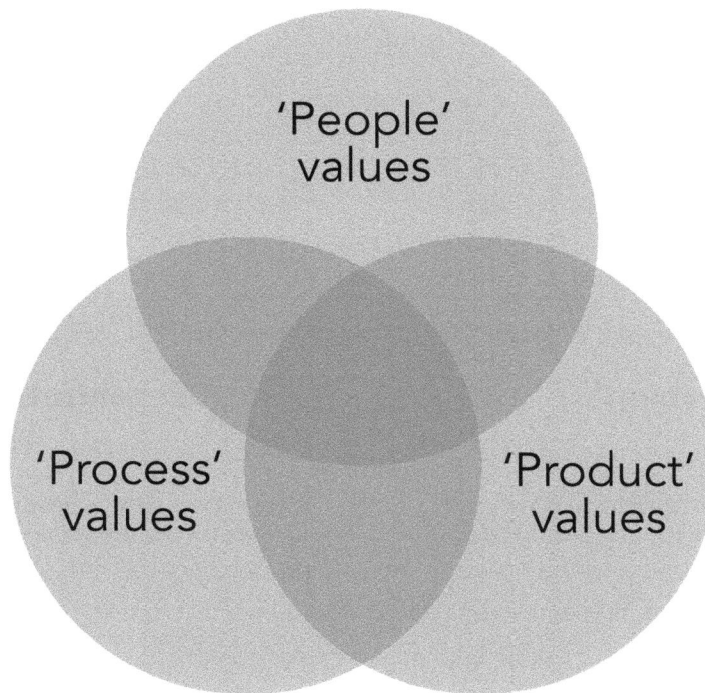

'People'
values

'Process'
values

'Product'
values

How you make decisions,
how you measure progress,
how you hold
people accountable

Which products you build,
how you respond to
threats and opportunities
in the market

Key purposes of core values

Taking a broad view of the potential purposes that core values could serve within an organisation suggests three axes along which these purposes could be positioned.

Three axes along which the purpose of core values could be positioned

What is the purpose of your core values, on this continuum?

'Maintainer' core values

These core values are designed to maintain your organisation as it is; to preserve its strengths and its heritage.

'Transformer' core values

These core values are designed to transform your organisation into something distinct from its current state.

What is the purpose of your core values, on this continuum?

'Personal meaning' core values

These are values intended to resonate with individuals across the organisation. They matter to me because they have personal meaning for me.

'Organisational utility' core values

These are values intended to serve the interests of the entire organisation. They matter because they enable us to work better as a whole.

What is the purpose of your core values, on this continuum?

'Place of work' core values

These core values affect our working lives and our ways of working.

'Place in the world' core values

These core values affect both how our place in the world is seen and how we make an impact in the world.

Key purposes of core values: Examples

Example #1: Scale-up business
"Our core values will be a key driver of us becoming more dynamic and innovative as a company over the coming 5 years. These values will aim to transform the attitudes and behaviours of our people, our teams and our leadership."
#transformer, #organisational-utility, #place-of-work

Example #2: Established family firm
"We are a successful family business, as we have been for the past 50 years and as we intend to be for the next 50. Part of our secret, we believe, is the endurance of our core family values – how the mutuality of our commitment is reflected by the mutuality of rewards for success." ***#maintainer, #personal-meaning.***

Example #3: Talent brand
"It is our core values that will make us the talent brand we seek to be. We will try to ensure every employee feels bought in to our purpose, our agenda for social good and our sense of belonging in the workplace."
#transformer, #place-of-work, #personal-meaning

Example #4: Climate charity
"Our organisation exists to mitigate the climate crisis facing planet Earth. We do so by campaigning and by providing practical advice to organisations seeking to reduce their environmental impact. Our core values guide our actions and inspire others to follow in our footsteps." ***#transformer, #place-in-the-world***

Example #5: University
"We seek to be a comprehensively research-led university. Our education will be shaped by the world's best pedagogic research. Our graduates will have experienced research and will appreciate its ways of working and its value for society. Our professional services will be innovative and will strive to match global best-practice in their service provision." ***#transformer, #place-in-the-world***

Note:
Make sure you avoid getting into defining core values here. There will be plenty of time for that later. Here, all we are doing is scoping.

Decide the audience for core values

Scoping core values – step #3

Deciding who your organisational values are for is a crucial, but frequently overlooked step. It may be because it seems so obvious – organisational values are for everyone in the organisation. A deeper analysis, however, reveals several more layers of complexity.

1. What about stakeholders that are external to your organisation? It might be good if your partners and suppliers adopted your core values.

2. What about your customers? For some organisations, their values determine their brand and hence a large part of their appeal to their customers. It's hard to imagine, for example, customers of ThredUp, the world's leading marketplace for secondhand fashion, not sharing its commitment to environmental sustainability.

3. What about the Board? Any significant mismatch between the values of the Board and the values of the rest of an organisation is likely to lead to conflict at some stage. Why not, therefore, include the Board as part of your target audience, when you scope your core values?

Audience definition is a key part of scoping organisational core values

Audience definition determines who core values are written for – who should we design them to be for?

Audience definition also determines what this audience (or these audiences, if plural) should be able to do with the core values.

Audience for Netflix's core values

In their famous 129-slide 'Culture Deck' from 2009, Netflix were very clear that some of their values applied only to some of their staff.

Freedom & Responsibility
Applies to our
Salaried Employees

Our hourly employees are important,
but have more structured job roles

NETFLIX

3

Netflix (2009)

Produce scoping statement

Scoping core values – step #4

Two examples:

Starting point: We have no core values. We never did. But we are growing rapidly. We can no longer depend on word-of-mouth to convey our values. We need to commit them to writing. These values need to align us – our decisions, our actions, our aspirations and our working relationships. We recognise this is a big ask and we may not get it right first time.

Purpose of core values: We have moved from being a start-up to being a scale-up. Our culture is, therefore, in the midst of a difficult transition. We must continue to be innovative but more narrowly innovative, having found product / market fit. We also need to standardise our ways of working to be able to scale effectively. Our values need to reflect this transition.

Audience for core values: For the next few years, our core values will be entirely for internal consumption (and possibly recruitment). We have no current plan to use our core values for branding or marketing.

Starting point: We have always had core values and they have always been important for us. But the world has moved on and they are no longer serving us well – we need to review and revise them.

Purpose of core values: We have been a successful family firm for over 70 years. Values have been important for us from the start and will continue to define us. These values, however, need to evolve. We are in the midst of a digital transformation of our entire business and need to introduce new values, such as digital-native, mobile-first, metrics-driven alongside our family-focused values.

Audience for core values: Our core values have always been a very public part of our business. We hope they are as important to our customers, partners and suppliers as they are to us within the company.

Devise / revise core values

You are now clear about the nature and purpose of core values in your organisation, possibly because you've just written a core values scoping statement.

So now you are good to get stuck into writing those core values. Here's how to tackle this process:

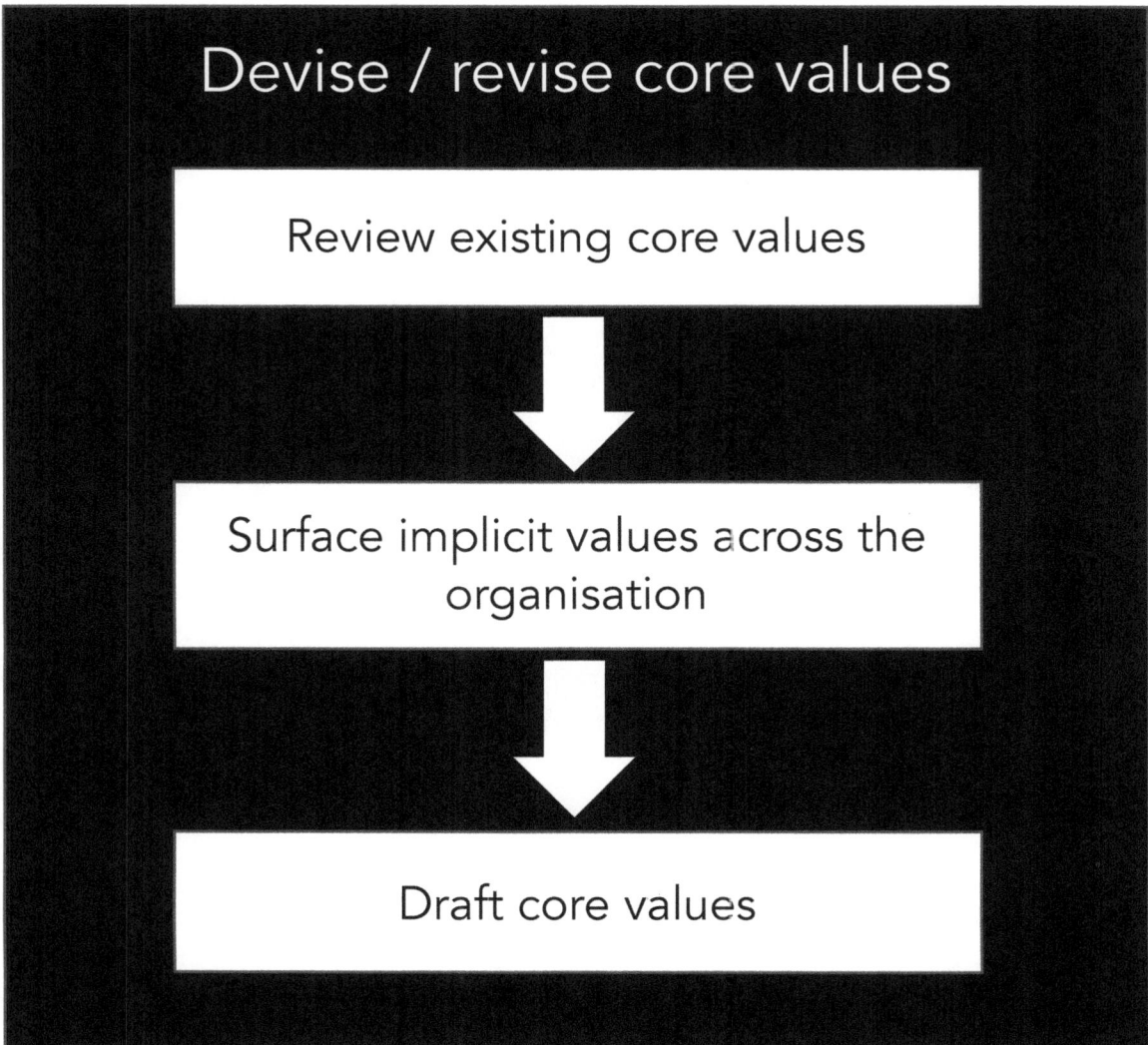

Devise / revise core values

Review existing core values

⬇

Surface implicit values across the organisation

⬇

Draft core values

The concepts of inventory and audit

As you move through the process of devising your core values, you may find the idea of a **values inventory** and a **values audit** useful.

An inventory is a highly structured, quantitative analysis of an organisation's assets and those asset's attributes.

An audit is an evaluation of the effectiveness of an organisation's assets and typically includes both quantitative and qualitative measures.

Both inventory and audit are applicable to the values of an organisation.

To conduct an **inventory** of organisational values, we need to find out what we currently have. What have we said previously about our values or our organisational culture? Also, what values are implicitly believed to apply to the organisation by the individuals working in it? The answer to both of these questions could be compiled into an inventory – what has been said or documented and what values do these statements appear to relate to?

To conduct an **audit** of organisational values, we begin by evaluating the values in our inventory. How well do these values reflect who we are and how we aspire to change? Can we prioritise these values in order of preference or utility? How well would these values serve us if we accepted them as our core values?

This audit process can then be revisited as we try to fill any perceived gaps in our values inventory – are there any values missing that we feel we ought to consider?

This process can then be revisited as many times as needed as we move from a long-list of candidate core values to a draft list of core values and then to a final list of articulated core values ready for launch across the organisation. Repeating this audit process, against similar audit criteria, gives continuity to the core values process and transparency to the decision-making along the way.

A key issue is, therefore, to decide on the criteria we will use for auditing our emerging core values and this is why we have just produced a scoping statement defining the purpose of having core values for our organisation – the audit criteria will be derived directly from this scoping statement.

Review existing core values

Devise / revise core values – step #1

Most organisations of significant size will have at least alluded to their core values within existing documentation: annual reports, strategy documents, policy papers, leadership presentations. They may not be called core values. Maybe 'core principles', or 'how we work' or 'what makes us different' or 'our culture'.

Wherever you find them, it is worth collecting together all references to core values. They can make great conversation starters. For example, in a workshop or town-hall meeting, the fact that your annual report from a couple of years ago highlighted 'teamwork' could be mentioned. "Do we think teamwork is something we either are, or ought to be, great at?", "In what ways do you see teamwork working really well in our organisation?", "Where do we need most improvement in our teamwork?", "Who sees 'teamwork' as a strong candidate to become one of our new core values?"

Inventory of organisational values

Through such discussions you will start to compile an inventory of the values you have found reference to. This inventory contains all the values that might possibly become part of what you subsequently commit to as your core values. Within reason, having lots of values in your inventory is good. This will enable you to evaluate the strengths and weaknesses of each. It will also enable you to be much more discriminating in your thinking about values. For example, your long-list might prompt you to think about what the difference is between 'diversity', 'inclusivity' and 'equality'. How would each of these values affect the decisions and actions we take as an organisation?

Remember, you are starting your inventory of organisational values from existing references to core values that your organisation has produced in the past. So, try to ensure you identify the source as well as the values they articulate.

Here are some examples of entries in a values inventory:

Value	Notes on value	Notes on source
Teamwork	'... teamwork has always been an important part of our culture'	CEO presentation to Board January 2019
Diversity	'... delighted to have reached our target of 40% women on our Board'	Annual Report 2021

Surface implicit values: principles

We all have values. Often, they are implicit: they are not talked about and people may not even know they exist. To bring them to the surface is to uncover them and make them explicit. There is even research suggesting that particular values are shared widely across 44 different countries, worldwide. These values, which Schwartz (1994) suggests are universal human values, are shown below.

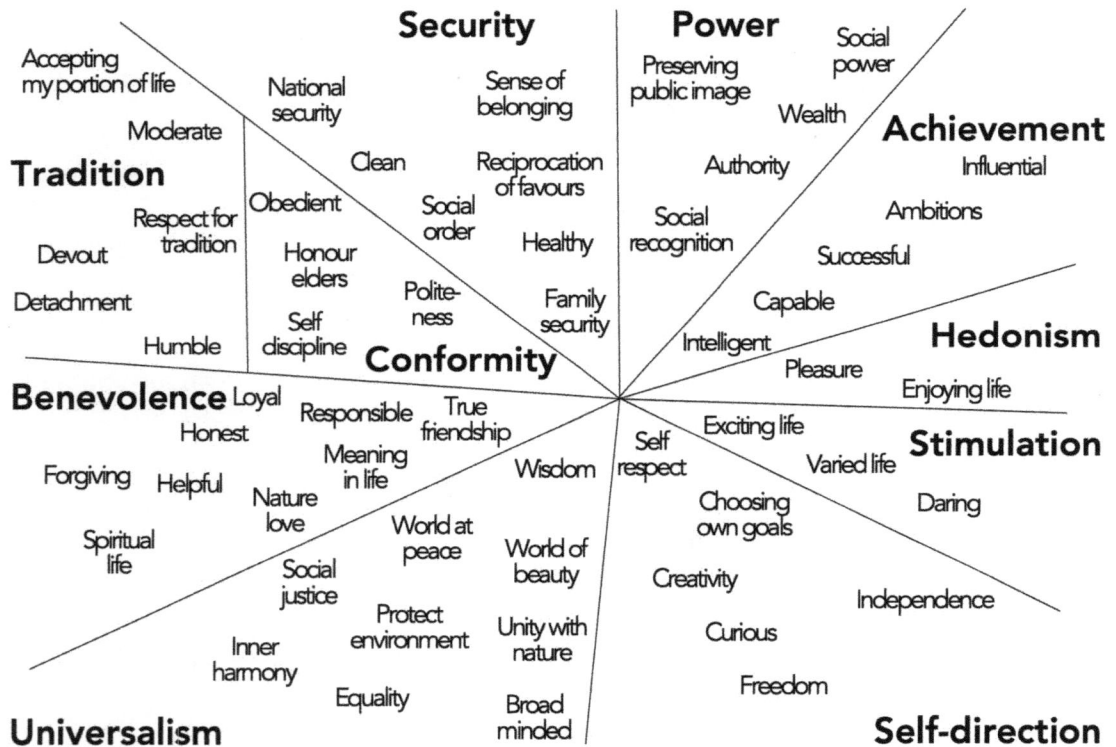

Security

Power

Social power

Accepting my portion of life

National security

Sense of belonging

Preserving public image

Wealth

Achievement

Moderate

Tradition

Clean

Reciprocation of favours

Authority

Influential

Obedient

Social order

Social recognition

Ambitions

Respect for tradition

Devout

Honour elders

Healthy

Successful

Detachment

Polite-ness

Family security

Capable

Hedonism

Humble

Self discipline

Conformity

Intelligent

Pleasure

Enjoying life

Benevolence Loyal

Responsible

True friendship

Exciting life

Self respect

Stimulation

Honest

Meaning in life

Wisdom

Varied life

Forgiving Helpful

Nature love

Choosing own goals

Daring

Spiritual life

Social justice

World at peace

World of beauty

Creativity

Independence

Protect environment

Unity with nature

Curious

Inner harmony

Freedom

Equality

Broad minded

Universalism

Self-direction

Values plotted using a Similarity Structure Analysis to reveal how close different values are to each other in meaning (from Schwartz, 1994, Figure 2).

Furthermore, the idea of moral projection has been discussed extensively in the business ethics literature (e.g. Goodpaster, 1987); individuals within organisations will ascribe values to that organisation, even when core values are not explicitly declared. So, surfacing implicit values within your organisation can often be highly informative in helping you devise a set of explicitly articulated core values.

Surface implicit values across the organisation

Devise / revise core values – step #2

To surface implicit values, the question you need answered is: what values do the individuals within our organisation feel best characterise us collectively? The answers need to come from a diverse enough sample of individuals to be representative of all parts of the organisation. In broad terms, there are two ways to ask this question, to ensure that the answers are useful.

1. **Unprompted** Ask the question directly but make sure you explain what organisational values are and what words are typically used to describe them. To put this in context, if you ask an individual employee about their values, they might explain that they live by Catholic values (or Muslim values or Hindu values). Unless your organisation has a specific religious affiliation, however, you are unlikely to include Catholic values in your organisation's core values. If this explanation is going to be sensitive or hard to get right, you might want to opt for a prompted approach instead.

2. **Prompted** Provide a list of the most commonly used organisational core values and ask people to select those they feel best characterise us, as an organisation. You may find the long-lists of organisational values in Appendix 2 useful for deriving prompts for your own organisation. As an option, you could also ask them to indicate their strength of feeling about different values. Be careful not to over-complicate this. A four-point scale should be sufficient:
   i.   Score +2 for all values that strongly characterise us as an organisation.
   ii. Score +1 for all values that slightly characterise us as an organisation.
   iii. Score -1 for all values that are slightly unlike us as an organisation.
   iv. Score -2 for all values that are strongly unlike us as an organisation.

In a large organisation, these questions will typically be asked in a survey, although the discussion of values will be richer and potentially more revealing if the questions are asked in series of meetings or workshops.

Now, let's move on to consider what you do with the results you get from surfacing implicit values across your organisation.

Inventory of values: example

Here is an example of a values inventory that you might produce from your review of existing values and your surfacing of implicit values.

Value	Notes on value	Source	Notes on source
Teamwork	'... teamwork has always been an important part of our culture'	Review of existing values	CEO presentation to Board January 2019
Diversity	'... delighted to have reached our target of 40% women on our Board'	Review of existing values	Annual Report 2021
Collaboration	'A critical failure in missing our launch date was the lack of collaboration between teams'	Review of existing values	After-project review June 2022
Integrity	Cited by 52 of 139 respondents to survey	Survey of implicit values	Rank #1 from 67 ranked responses to survey
Innovation	Cited by 39 of 139 respondents to survey	Survey of implicit values	Rank #2 from 67 ranked responses to survey
Accountability	Cited by 79 of 139 respondents to survey	Survey of implicit values	Rank #3 from 67 ranked responses to survey
Environmental sustainability	Cited by 27 of 139 respondents to survey	Survey of implicit values	Rank #4 from 67 ranked responses to survey
Agility	Cited by 44 of 139 respondents to survey	Survey of implicit values	Rank #5 from 67 ranked responses to survey

From inventory to audit: example

Here is an example of how the inventory of values that you just completed could be audited.

Notes on inventory of values

Our strategy over the next three years is to reposition ourselves in the marketplace by means of new product development. It is, therefore, great to see innovation as one of the top-ranked values in the survey. It is also significant that our failure to collaborate effectively is picked up in the review. Innovation and collaboration are therefore two values we need to explore in more depth.

Cluster analysis

Here are the values with similar meanings to innovation and collaboration:

Risk taking

Curiosity   Creativity

Innovation

Test, test, test   Agility

Ambition/boldness

Transparency

Respect   Accountability

Collaboration

Trust   Honesty

Communication

Reflections

Reflections on 'Innovation'

We don't seem to be lacking in good ideas. Where we struggle is translating them into successful products. We need to engage customers a lot more and a lot earlier in the process. To do so we need to get better at prototyping, so we have something to test with customers. This certainly does seem to be a cultural issue. Our mindset seems to disappear into a darkened room and only come out when the new product is finished. This needs to change.

Reflections on 'Collaboration'

We work in silos far too much. This may be a consequence of senior leaders, in the past, holding departmental managers to account only for their departmental performance. Now our strategy will only succeed as a result of work crossing departmental boundaries. This will only happen if we instil a culture of collaboration. The above cluster analysis suggests there may be two key components: 1 good communication & transparency and 2. honesty, trust & respect.

Draft core values

Devise / revise core values – step #3

This is our first step towards a commitment to a specific set of core values for the organisation. It should aim to achieve three outcomes:

1. Propose, for the first time, what or new core values ought to be;
2. Explain the thinking behind this proposal and the anticipated benefits of these particular core values;
3. Explore how these core values are expected to work together and any synergies that might result from them working in harmony.

Here are example draft core values for 'innovation' and 'collaboration' that we've just audited.

Proposed core values	
Innovation	**Collaboration**
Background	
We already do a lot of innovation. We just need to do it better and this should happen if we engage customers a lot more and a lot earlier in the process.	Since strategic success depends on our work crossing departmental boundaries, we need to be more collaborative. We need better communication and ways to build better working relationships.
Making an impact	
We could start with a pilot project – something quick but impactful to explore the practicalities of innovation with more customer-engagement. Then roll our learnings out on a major innovation program. We will also need to tighten up our tracking of innovation initiatives.	Let's start at the top and work through the whole organisation. Let's get two or three of the senior team publicly committed to working on a high-profile collaborative project. They can then bring their teams in to work together as and when they are needed.
Synergies	
These two core values could work brilliantly together – we maybe need to tweak the collaboration core value so that it includes collaborating with customers.	

Articulate & apply core values

You now have a set of draft core values for your organisation

Now you need to decide how they are going to be articulated, launched and applied. Here are the steps in this process:

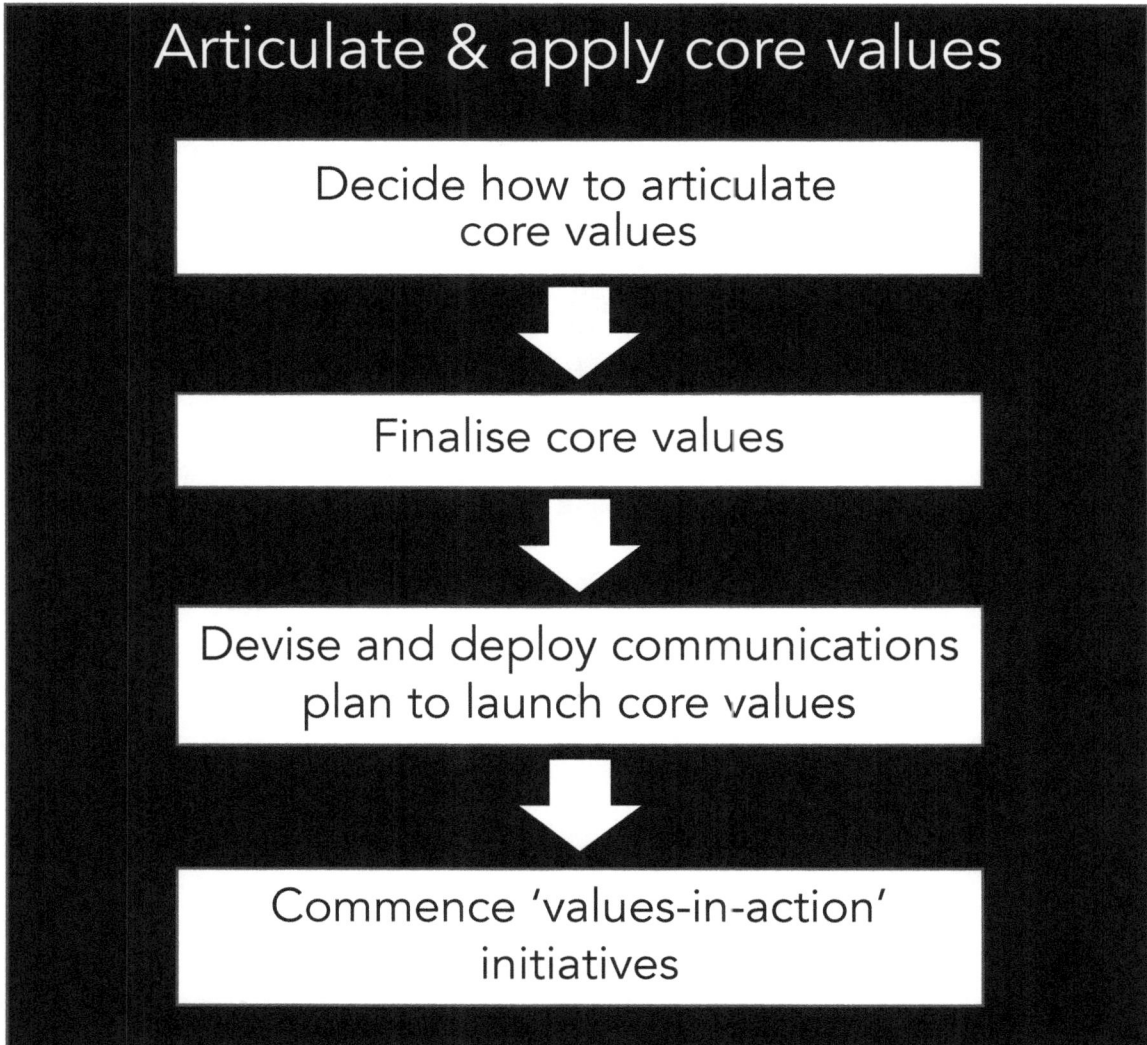

Articulate & apply core values

Decide how to articulate core values

⬇

Finalise core values

⬇

Devise and deploy communications plan to launch core values

⬇

Commence 'values-in-action' initiatives

Delphi survey method for core values

Introduction
Devising, articulating and applying core values is often a complex process that combines executive decision-making with widespread consultation and discussion across the whole organisation. Delphi technique can help streamline this entire process.

What is Delphi technique?
"The Delphi technique is a scientific method to organize and manage structured group communication processes with the aim of generating insights on either current or prospective challenges; especially in situations with limited availability of information ... it has been frequently used in various scientific disciplines ranging from health care, medicine, education, business, engineering and technology ..." Beiderbeck et al (2021)

Step #1 The core values working group Appoint a core values working group. This should include members of your leadership team, your people team and any other individuals with a specialist understanding of, or interest in, core values for the organisation. Group size is typically 5 to 30 people. Draw up (usually written) terms of reference for the group, derived from your core values scoping statement.

Step #2 Core values long-list The working group produces an initial long-list of potential core values. Sometimes the working group will do this themselves, perhaps based on previously published value statements. Alternatively, they may want to derive it from a staff survey. After sharing all source material, each member of the working group submits an anonymous proposal of no more than 10 core values.

Step #3 Draft set of core values The working group reviews the proposals and produces a draft set of core values. These core values must reflect both the implicit core values currently 'felt' by the organisation and the purposes that these core values are intended to serve. Staff views on this draft set of core values is then sought by means of another survey.

Step #4 Published final set of core values Based on this next round of feedback the working group publishes a final set of core values, making clear the process by which they have been produced.

Articulating core values: a cautionary tale

It is all too tempting for leadership, especially for a new CEO, just appointed to the role, to imagine they can command a new set of core values into existence. There are, however, far too many stories of this being attempted and failing for this to be your best approach.

> " When [Camillo Pane] took over Coty Inc. in 2016, Pane publicly declared that the struggling fragrance and cosmetics giant needed to begin 'acting like a startup' and 'adopt a challenger mentality'. For all that rhetoric, nothing about Coty's culture or performance changed in the two years following Pane's appointment and he was fired in 2018. "

(Martin, 2022, p.96)

Decide how to articulate core values

Articulate & apply core values – step #1

Refresher

In Part 2 we reviewed different presentation formats for core values.

Single word label e.g. Innovative

Paired values e.g. Innovative & enterprising

Themed values e.g. Fostering innovation and creativity

Descriptive value statements e.g. Actively seek opportunities for innovation and strive to exploit them creatively and profitably

Decision- and action-oriented values e.g. Enterprising creativity: we're adaptable, flexible, and consider a fresh approach in everything we do. We are innovative and open to change. We work with, learning from, and share with others. We look outside our own environment to find solutions to problems. We use constructive feedback and regularly looking to improve the way we do things.

We seek to deliberately change the decision-making and actions across the organisation by means of these core values. We will, therefore, emphasise the decision- and action-oriented format for our core values. Having reviewed the published core values of several other organisations, the features best suited to our needs is as follows:

<Single word label for core value, with icon>
<Concise, punchy, action-oriented explanation of the core value>

This means ... <describe the decisions, actions and consequences>	Our commitment is that we will <what we'll do that's new>	Our commitment is that we will not <what we'll stop that we used to do>
Over the course of <number of months / years> we will know we will have succeeded because we will have <evidence of change sought>		

Example

Customer-centric innovation
Innovation that customers love because they were involved from the start.

This means we will engage customers at all stages of our innovations.	Our commitment is to test all new ideas with customers and listen to what they think.	Our commitment is that we will stop assuming we always know best.
Over the course of the next 18 months we will know we will have succeeded because our products will sell well from the moment they are launched.		

Having decided the format for your core values, there are a couple of other decisions to be made about their articulation:

1. **What are you going to call them?** The obvious answer is to call them 'core values'. This has the great advantage that they will have an intrinsic and common-sense meaning. Remember our definition from *'the basics of core values'* in Part 1: **the 'core values' of an organisation are 'the shared principles and beliefs which guide the decisions and actions of everyone across the organisation'.** However, not everyone agrees. Google has a 'philosophy' containing a set of things that are remarkably values-like and they call them 'Ten things we know to be true'. Amazon's equivalent is a list of sixteen 'Leadership principles'. Mars has 'Five Principles' that 'form the foundation of how we do business today and every day'. When launching their values in 2015, Twilio rejected the label 'core values' and instead went for 'Our 9 things' (Lawson, 2015). More recently, they reverted to conformity – they now have 'Values' (Twilio, 2023). There is maybe a lesson here for all of us. Call them 'core values' unless you have a very good reason not to.

2. **What do you say to introduce your core values?** It is probably a good idea to explain what you want everyone to do with them. You could explain that they are shared principles and beliefs which guide the decisions and actions of everyone across the organisation (as it says in the above definition). You could also explain what is NOT intended by them. They are not, for example, a demand that every individual's personal values conform. You do not need to proclaim the organisation's core values as your own in order to work here. They are also not a camouflaged attack on diversity. There will be no check-box confirming adherence to each and every core value by each new employee, from this day on. Indeed, Melissa Daimler, chief learning officer of Udemy suggests that new employees should "bring a different set of perspectives that stil complement who we are and what we're doing as a company. We can't continue to grow and be innovative if we don't have additional perspectives on our team" (Daimler, 2022).

Finalise core values

Articulate & apply core values – step #2

Finalising your core values

Having drafted your core values and then decided how to articulate them, it should now be relatively straightforward to finalise them. Also, now that you know what's in them and what impact they are hoped to have across the organisation, you should also be clear about who should sign them off and be held accountable for their success. Typically this will be the CEO, with the Board being informed of their official sign-off.

Nike's manifesto from 1980

This doesn't look like a conventional statement of core values, yet its underlying values shine through clearly (Nike 1980)

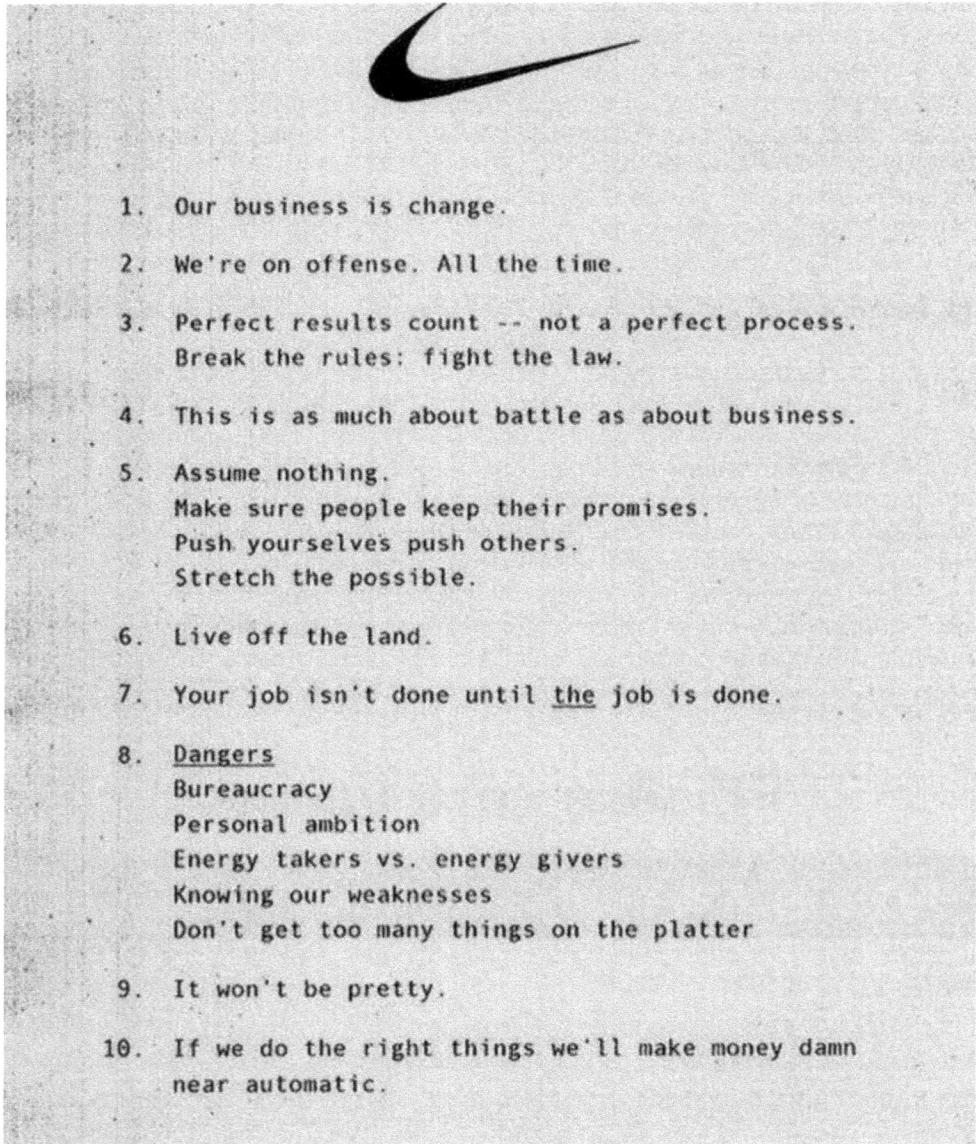

1. Our business is change.

2. We're on offense. All the time.

3. Perfect results count -- not a perfect process.
   Break the rules: fight the law.

4. This is as much about battle as about business.

5. Assume nothing.
   Make sure people keep their promises.
   Push yourselves push others.
   Stretch the possible.

6. Live off the land.

7. Your job isn't done until the job is done.

8. Dangers
   Bureaucracy
   Personal ambition
   Energy takers vs. energy givers
   Knowing our weaknesses
   Don't get too many things on the platter

9. It won't be pretty.

10. If we do the right things we'll make money damn
    near automatic.

Devise and deploy communication plan to launch core values

Articulate & apply core values – step #3

Your brand new core values are now ready for launch and roll-out across the organisation. Here are some of the key components you should think about including in your communication plan.

Components of a communication plan for core values

1. **Audience** Core values are usually published for both internal and external audiences. A dedicated web page is the usual place to put them.

2. **Key messages** If the core values are part of a broader strategy or change program, clear messaging will be needed to make this clear, including what action is expected by whom and by when.

3. **Publication** Which formats, media and channels are these core values going to be published on? Website, intranet, in-house messaging / social media? What about print? Posters in meeting rooms? Table-mats in eating spaces and coffee rooms?

4. **Launch event(s)** Will there be a specific event to herald the launch of the new core values? If so, think carefully about who should be involved. Just the CEO? Might be seen as too top-down. Are these values that leadership is seeking to impose on the rest of us? Maybe have a representative group from across the organisation launch them? Try to show they are a genuine grass-roots initiative. Without the CEO being present? Probably not – it's good to show that the core values have the support of senior leadership.

5. **Post launch events** Do individuals and groups need support to align their working practices to these new values? Do any conflicts arise for anyone (e.g. new core values clash with existing policy documents)? Should we plan any 'town hall' sessions to review progress with the new core values and celebrate successes?

Commence 'values in action' initiatives

Articulate & apply core values – step #4

You need to be clear about what is going to happen to these new core values, once they are launched. What, at a practical level is going to be different? It is always great for senior leaders to 'light the path' by clarifying what they personally are going to do differently in response to these core values.

Ideally, you will have a comprehensive plan of who needs to do what in response to your new core values in order for them to have their intended impact. The depth and complexity of this plan will inevitably vary hugely for different organisations in different circumstances.

There is a big difference between 'proclaimed values' and 'actioned values'.

Proclaimed values are what we talk about but don't actually do. They are cultural window-dressing.

Actioned values, on the other hand are the ones we use for decisions and actions. Even although we may not talk about them much, they become implicit in our ways of working.

Always make sure, when devising and applying your core values, that they are the 'actioned' variety, not just 'proclaimed'.

Values in action from Minecraft

Minecraft, one of the biggest selling games of all time, recently decided to exclude non-fungible tokens (NFTs) because they 'don't align with Minecraft values'. Here is an excerpt from their announcement (Minecraft, 2022):

"[Using] NFTs and other blockchain technologies creates digital ownership based on scarcity and exclusion, which does not align with Minecraft values of creative inclusion and playing together. NFTs are not inclusive of all our community and create a scenario of the haves and the have-nots. The speculative pricing and investment mentality around NFTs takes the focus away from playing the game and encourages profiteering, which we think is inconsistent with the long-term joy and success of our players."

Patagonia on values

> *People often choose to do the right thing, not strictly as a business decision, but on the basis of values. They may be shy about talking about values as a basis for action, but I think it's very common and can build strong business relationships. We've found a lot of partners that way.*

Vincent Stanley, Director of Philosophy, Patagonia

Track & refine core values

Your core values are now launched, or at least ready to launch.

Now you need to decide how they are going to be tracked, risk managed and reviewed.

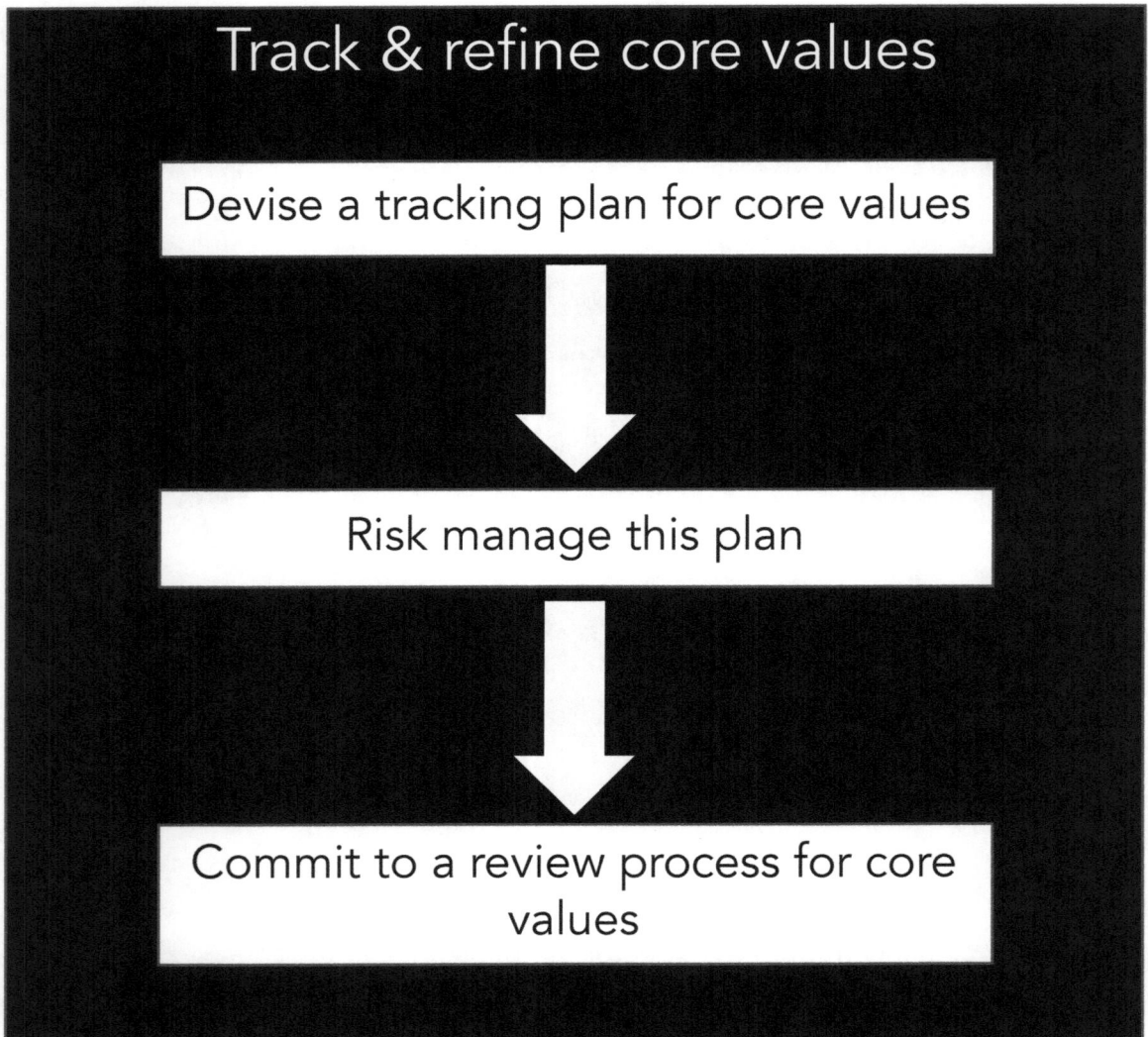

Track & refine core values

Devise a tracking plan for core values

↓

Risk manage this plan

↓

Commit to a review process for core values

Devise a tracking plan for core values

Track & refine core values – step #1

Do you track core values separately or is their impact measured as part of other analytic processes? Whilst there can never be a single universal answer to such a question, there is a compelling logic pointing in a specific direction.

If core values are worth all the effort needed to devise them, articulate them and launch them, they must surely be of considerable value to the organisation. And, indeed, they do appear to be valuable for shaping and aligning the decision-making and actions of individuals and teams across the organisation. So, if they are this valuable, surely they must be worth tracking and reviewing?

Tracking core values

Many organisations find it useful to think of two tracking processes, happening at different levels in the organisation, for core values.

1. **Formative tracking** monitors how core values are working to provide ongoing feedback that can be used to improve how they are being interpreted and applied. Formative tracking usually is done by front-line teams, departments or business units. Here's how this type of tracking usually works, as part of performance management conversations between you and your line manager. Raise the topic of core values. Explore possible stretch goals derived from the core values – what new ways of working that seem better aligned with core values you could try out. Agree a tangible target - your stretch goal. This could be adopting a new process, trying to manage specific working relationships differently or simply thinking about an aspect of your work in a new light. Commit to a clearly defined decision or action over an agreed timescale and ask clearly if you need any support or facilitation from your manager for this stretch goal. Note what you anticipate the impact will be and agree a date in the not-too-distant future when you will review how it worked. If it works, try a bigger stretch next time. If it didn't work, reflect on why, how to do better next time and give it another go.

2. **Summative tracking** attempts to sum all evidence of the impact of core values across the entire organisation to determine how effectively they have worked. Summative tracking of core values is ultimately done by, or on behalf of, the senior leadership team. There are three main approaches to summative tracking of core values:
   - Lagging indicators – decide what beneficial impact core values ought to have for the organisation and set out to measure this impact after it has had time to take effect.
   - Aggregation – try to aggregate all the formative tracking outcomes (usually leading indicators) by getting line managers to report upwards.
   - Dedicated online culture tracking tools, such as CultureAmp or CultureIQ .

Risk manage the tracking plan for core values

Track & refine core values – step #2

It is all too easy to see core values in an exclusively positive light. They are the principles and beliefs that bring us together, amplify what we have in common and bring our actions into alignment. This, however, is not always the case. Core values can come into conflict with one another. Some core values can be applied in extreme ways that can be seen as offensive or hateful.

Managing core values well, requires that we try to anticipate the challenges that might arise and the risks that we may need to mitigate or manage. Including a risk analysis in tracking and review processes can help to identify changing risks and the steps that may need to be taken to address them effectively.

Here are some examples of core values that may need to be risk managed:

Examples

Core value: Excellence
Potential risks to address: How do we stop this turning into elitism? Which aspects of excellence are we referring to? Do we, for example, only recruit graduates from the highest ranking universities? What do we seek to do about excellence? Are we, for example, making a commitment to eliminate anyone or anything that falls short of excellence from the organisation?

Core value: Freedom of speech
Potential risks to address: What are the limits on freedom of speech, if any? Speech inciting hatred or violence is illegal in the UK. But what about speech that makes minority or vulnerable groups feel unsafe or unsupported?

Core value: Equality
Potential risks to address: How do we go about rectifying inequalities. Do we, for example, tolerate bias against an over-represented majority in order to increase an under-represented minority?

Core value: Innovation
Potential risks to address: Where does the boundary lie between innovation that is seen as a 'good bet' for an organisation and innovation that is a 'bad bet'.

Core value: Accountability
Potential risks to address: When does holding someone to account turn into harassment? How is the right balance struck between 'holding to account' and 'supporting to succeed'?

Commit to a review process for core values

Track & refine core values – step #3

Step 1: Devise a review process, based on the purpose of your core values. How quickly do you expect the impact of core values to be seen? If you are trying to be a more innovative organisation, there may be nothing to review for many months. If, on the other hand, you are committing to more collaborative ways of working, you could see a difference in a few weeks. So, pick a review cycle appropriate to the expected impact of your new core values.

Step 2: Decide who is going to do the reviewing. Ultimately the senior leadership team for the whole organisation should review how core values are working in the run-up to the annual planning and budgeting round. This way, if investment is required to boost the impact of core values, it can be incorporated into next year's plans. There may need to be a series of departmental or functional reviews feeding into the senior leadership review of core values. These might look at different aspects of core values or simply explore what impact they are having in different parts of the organisation.

Step 3: Be clear, at the start, what success and failure are going to look like at the end of the first (and subsequent) years. Try to be stretching in your aspirations but realistic in your evaluations. After all, core values are there to make a difference.

Concluding remarks

There is no doubt that core values and organisational culture lie on the softer side of management science. For many leaders, they are such soft topics that they are not taken seriously and are paid lip-service, if they are addressed at all.

What I hope comes across loud and clear from this book is that core values can be made sense of in a structured and systematic way. Perhaps even more importantly, they can be managed with a deliberate and highly procedural workflow.

This doesn't make them easy to devise, to articulate, to apply or to track but it does bring them into the usual orbit of leaders, managers and front-line teams. They can be brought into existence without magic or mystery. They can be applied in ways that the organisation might welcome and applaud. And they can have impact that would bring joy to the heart of the most process-focused, metrics-driven of CEOs.

It will be a challenging journey for you, but with tools and processes like the ones we've covered in this book, it is a navigable journey and one with a reachable destination.

Bon voyage!

References

Allen J, 2022. Clear corporate values underpin everything you do as an organisation. They say why you exist and how you want to do business. *Creative Huddle Blog* 29 December 2022. https://www. creativehuddle.co.uk/post/how-company-core-values-can-help-align-your-people-to-your-goals.

Amazon, 2023. *Leadership Principles.* https://www.aboutamazon.com/about-us/leadership-principles.

Azoulay J, 2017. *Bullshit values, actionable values: the talent.io experience.* https://medium.com/@Jon_ Azoulay/bullshit-values-actionable-values-the-talent-io-experience-582cf62498f5

Barnett R, 2022. *The Philosophy of Higher Education.* Routledge, London.

Baxter M, 2019. *University Strategy 2020: Analysis and benchmarking of the strategies of UK universities.* Goal Atlas, London.

Baxter M, 2020. *House of Strategy Model* https://goalatlas.com/house-of-strategy/.

Baxter M, 2020. *The Strategy Manual: A step-by-step guide to the transformational change of anything.* Goal Atlas, London.

Becker BE, 2001. Quote from Becker BE, Huselid MA and & Ulrich D, 2001. Making HR a Strategic Asset. *Financial Times*, November, 2001.

Beiderbeck D, Frevel N, von der Gracht HA, Schmidt SL and Schweitzer VM, 2021. Preparing, conducting, and analyzing Delphi surveys: Cross-disciplinary practices, new directions, and advancements. *Methods X* 8: 101401. https://methods-x.com/article/S2215-0161(21)00194-1/fulltext.

Bezos J, 2012. Quote retrieved from George Anders, Jeff Bezos's Top 10 Leadership Lessons. *Forbes* 4 April 2012. https://www.forbes.com/sites/georgeanders/2012/04/04/bezos-tips/?sh=4ba528492fce

Biogen, 2023. *Elements of our culture.* https://www.biogen.com/company/culture-elements.html.

Butterfield S, 2015. Stewart Butterfield of Slack: Is empathy on your resume? *New York Times* 12 July 2015. https://www.nytimes.com/2015/07/12/business/stewart-butterfield-of-slack-experience-with-empathy-required.html.

Daimler M, 2022. *Author Talks: Don't skip the 'soft stuff.* https://www.mckinsey.com/featured-insights/ mckinsey-on-books/author-talks-dont-skip-the-soft-stuff.

Daschle A, Jurisic N, Parsons J and Varma R, 2019. Set your cultural aspiration with these four steps. *McKinsey Organisation Blog.* July 2019. https://www.mckinsey.com/capabilities/people-and-organizational-performance/our-insights/the-organization-blog/set-your-cultural-aspiration-with-these-four-steps

DeMille CB, 2009. Quote retrieved from Sabile Klocker 2009, *Manual for Facilitators in Non-formal Education Involved in Preparing and Delivering the Programme of Study Sessions at European Youth Centres*. Council of Europe, p13.

Disney R, 2019. Quote retrieved from Lee Colan, A lesson from Roy A Disney on making values based decisions. *Inc.com* 24 July 2019. https://www.inc.com/lee-colan/a-lesson-from-roy-a-disney-on-making-values-based-decisions.html.

Forsyth B, 2015. Quote retrieved from George Dickson, Shopify's Brittany Forsyth on Scaling Company Culture. *Bonus.ly Blog* https://blog.bonus.ly/shopifys-brittany-forsyth-on-scaling-culture/

Goodpaster K, 1987. The Principle of Moral Projection: A Reply to Professor Ranken. *Journal of Business Ethics*, 6 (4): 329-332.

Google, 2023. *Ten things we know we to be true*. https://about.google/philosophy/

Google Trends, 2023. *Analysis of 'people strategy' from 01 Jan 2019 to 31 Dec 2022*. https://trends.google.com/trends/explore?date=2019-01-01%202022-12-31&geo=GB&q=people%20strategy.

Grant A, 2015. The one question you should ask about any new job. *New York Times*, 20 Dec 2015. https://www.nytimes.com/2015/12/20/opinion/sunday/the-one-question-you-should-ask-about-every-new-job.html

Guiso L, Sapienza P and Zingales L, 2015. The value of corporate culture. *Journal of Financial Economics* 117 (1): 60-76.

Hedges C, 2020. *The politics of cultural despair*. https://canadiandimension.com/articles/view/the-politics-of-cultural-despair

Hsieh T, 2010. *Delivering Happiness: A Path to Profits, Passion, and Purpose*. Business Plus Publishing, NY.

Jobs S, 2018. Quote retrieved from Oren Ziv, Manage the Top Line. *Oren Ziv Blog* 26 May 2018. https://www.orenziv.com/blog/2018/6/27/manage-the-top-li.

Lawson J, 2015. *Articulating Company Values & Living Them Authentically*. https://www.youtube.com/watch?v=0CKl8Jah-Po.

Lencioni P, 2002. Make your values mean something. *Harvard Business Review*, July 2002.

Mars, 2023. *Five Principles*. https://www.mars.com/about/five-principles

Martin R, 2022. *A New Way to Think*, Harvard Business Review Press, Boston.

Minecraft, 2022. *Minecraft and NFTs*. https://www.minecraft.net/en-us/article/minecraft-and-nfts.

Netflix, 2009. *Culture (Original Version, 2009) by Reed Hastings*. https://www.slideshare.net/reed2001/culture-2009.

Nike, 1980. *Nike's Manifesto*. Retrieved from @mrexits (2023) https://twitter.com/mrexits/status/1614437652438319104

Pigneur Y, 2017. https://twitter.com/AlexOsterwalder/status/827887438211203072.

Schein EH, 1990. Organizational culture. *American Psychologist*, 45(2), 109–119.

Schwartz SH, 1994. Are there universal aspects in the structure and content of human values? *Journal of Social Issues* 50 (4): 19-45.

Sinek S, 2014. https://twitter.com/simonsinek/status/456545886143643649?lang=en

Smith ME, 2003. Changing an organisation's culture: correlates of success and failure. *Leadership and Organization Development Journal*, 24 (5): 249-261

Stern F, 1961. *The Politics Of Cultural Despair: A Study In The Rise Of The Germanic Ideology*, University of California Press, Berkeley.

Stewart J, 2009. Quote from *The Daily Show* January 22 2009. https://www.azquotes.com/quote/377732.

Stanley V, 2021. How Patagonia Learned to Act on Its Values. *Yale Insights*. https://insights.som.yale.edu/insights/how-patagonia-learned-to-act-on-its-values.

Sull D and Sull C, 2021. 10 Things Your Corporate Culture Needs to Get Right. *MIT Sloan Management Review,* 16 September 2021. https://sloanreview.mit.edu/article/10-things-your-corporate-culture-needs-to-get-right/.

Sull D, Turconi S, and Sull C, 2020. When It Comes to Culture, Does Your Company Walk the Talk? *MIT Sloan Management Review,* 21 July 2020 https://sloanreview.mit.edu/article/when-it-comes-to-culture-does-your-company-walk-the-talk/.

Twilio, 2023. *The Twilio Magic is our defining spirit.* https://www.twilio.com/company/values.

University of Birmingham, 2021. *2030 Strategic Framework.* https://www.birmingham.ac.uk/documents/strategic-framework/birmingham-2030-strategic-framework-accessible.docx.

Welch J, 2013. Quote retrieved from Laura Stack, The Ultimate Competitive Advantage: Translating Learning into Action. *The Productivity Pro Blog,* 5 August 2013. https://theproductivitypro.com/blog/2013/08/the-ultimate-competitive-advantage-translating-learning-into-action/.

Appendix 1: University values research

University Strategy 2030: Values Research

36 university strategies were considered for this research, all dating to 2030 or beyond. The values statements in their strategies were analysed between October 2022 and January 2023 using their own published online resources (webpages and pdfs) available at that time. This analysis is part of a broader research project (University Strategy 2030) currently being undertaken by Goal Atlas.

Data was taken from the following universities:

1.   Arts University Bournemouth

2.   Bangor University

3.   Bath Spa University

4.   Brunel University London

5.   Coventry University

6.   Falmouth University

7.   Glasgow Caledonian University

8.   Loughborough University

9.   Manchester Metropolitan University

10.   Middlesex University

11.   Oxford Brookes University

12.   Queen Mary University of London

13.   Queen's University Belfast

14.   St Mary's University, Twickenham

15.   Staffordshire University

16.   The London School of Economics and Political Science

17.   University College London

18.   University of Aberdeen

19.   University of Birmingham

20.   University of Bristol

21.   University of Derby

22.   University of East Anglia

23.   University of Edinburgh

24.   University of Exeter

25.   University of Greenwich

26.   University of Hull

27.   University of Leeds

28.   University of Plymouth

29.   University of South Wales

30.   University of Suffolk

31.   University of the Arts London

32.   University of the West of England, Bristol

33.   University of Warwick

34.   University of Winchester

35.   University of Wolverhampton

36.   University of York

Of these 36:

- 27 had a section described, in various ways as 'values' (Values [6], Our values [16], Our core values [1], Our values and guiding principles [1], Values and responsibility [1], Our mission & values [1], Shared values [1])

- five had a section described, in various ways, as 'principles' (Principles [1], Guiding Principles [2], Core Principles [1], Community Principles [1])

- three had a narrative description in their strategy that included explicit statements that could be considered as values / guiding principles (e.g. "Above all, life at Warwick will be underpinned by an unchanging set of values based on openness, diversity, respect and trust.")

- one strategy had no explicit statement of values or principles (this is not to say that there were no implicit values, however this strategy was excluded from further analysis).

For those with a section under the title 'values' or 'principles' (n=32):

- 28 had labels with a single word (e.g. sustainability) or a few words (e.g. collaboration across multidisciplinary boundaries)

- four had a narrative description only

- 22 of those with single/few word labels had a further narrative description under each label, as illustrated with this example from the University of Hull:

We are *inclusive*

- We provide a safe, friendly and welcoming environment for all, where our differences are celebrated

- We help each and every one of our students, staff and partners to achieve their full potential with a personal, supportive approach

- We celebrate individual and collective success

- We are mindful as to the positive and negative impact of what we each do, every day, on other individuals and communities both near and far

The number of single/few word labels ranged from 3 to 10, with most (12 out of 28) having 4 terms, and 89% (25 out of 28) having between 3 and 5 terms (mean=4.6), as shown in Fig. 1 below.

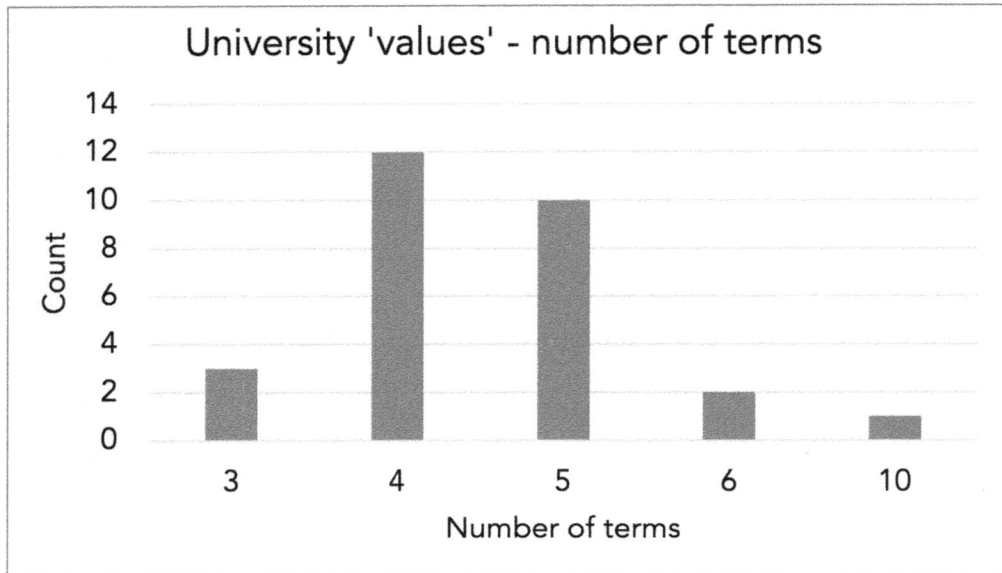

Figure 1. Number of single/few word labels for 'Values' in 28 university strategies analysed (with 2030 or beyond end dates).

The 28 strategies with labelled values / principles were analysed and collated into groups of similar terms (e.g. collaborative, collaboration). The top terms are shown in Table 1, compared to the top terms in the University Strategy 2020 report, and as a tag cloud in Figure 2.

Other values used in 2030+ university strategies included:
Adventurousness; Authenticity; Boldness; Brilliance; Caring; Community; Confidence; Curiousity; Daring; Determination; Discovery; Empowerment; Ethical; Future-focused; Generosity of spirit; Honesty; Impact; Inspiring; Internationalism; Openness; People-led; Pride; Professionalism; Progressiveness; Quality; Reputation; Responsibility; Responsiveness; Simplicity; Spirituality; Student-centred; Transformative.

See Appendix 2 for a list of 68 values cited (explicitly or in narrative) by the universities in this analysis.

Table 1: Comparison of University Strategy 2020 and Core Values (2030+) values terms

Data for University Strategy 2020 report

Value	Number of times mentioned in values labels in 24 university strategies
Inclusion	13
Excellence	12
Ambition	10
Integrity	7
Innovation	6
Professionalism[†]	6
Respect	6
Collaboration	5
Community[†]	4
Creativity	4
Diversity	4
Fairness	4
Sustainability	4
Collegiality	3
Openness	3
Responsibility	3

Data for Core Values (2030+)

Value	Number of times mentioned in values labels in 28* university strategies
Inclusion	17
Collaboration	11
Creativity	8
Ambition	7
Innovation	6
Integrity	6
Respect	6
Excellence	5
Diversity	4
Sustainability	4
Collegiality	3
Connectedness[‡]	3
Enterprise[‡]	3
Equality[‡]	3
Fairness	3
Openness	3
Responsibility	3

* Universities with 2030+ end date, not the same list as for 2020 report

[†] Not in top terms for Core Values report

[‡] Not in top terms for University Strategy 2020 report

Figure 2. Tag cloud for top values terms in 2030+ strategies

Appendix 2: Lists of values

Long-list of values cited by corporations (from Sull et al 2020)

Accountability
Agility
Ambition/boldness
Authenticity
Brand
Candid discussions
Caring
Change
Civility
Collaboration
Continuous improvement
Courage
Creativity
Curiosity
Customer
Data based
Diversity
Efficiency
Empathy
Empowerment
Entrepreneurial
Excellence
Execution
Expertise
Fairness
Financial returns
Fun
Growth
Health
Honesty
Humility

Independence
Innovation
Integrity
Leadership
Learning
Long-term view
Loyalty
Partnerships
Passion
People
Performance
Perseverance
Positive attitude
Pride
Professionalism
Quality
Respect
Responsibility
Risk management
Safety
Service
Simplicity
Social responsibility
Speed
Stewardship
Take risks
Transparency
Trust
Value
Winning
Work ethic

Long-list of values cited by universities (from this research see Appendix 1)

Accessibility
Achievement
Action
Adventurousness
Ambition
Authenticity
Boldness
Braveness
Brilliance
Caring
Challenge
Collaboration
Collegiality
Community
Compassion
Confidence
Connectedness
Consideration
Creativity
Curiosity
Daring
Determination
Discovery
Diversity
Effectiveness
Empowerment
Engagement
Enterprise
Environmental sustainability
Equality
Ethical
Excellence
Fairness
Freedom of thought

Future-focused
Generosity of spirit
Honesty
Impact
Inclusion
Innovation
Inspiring
Integrity
Interdisciplinary
Internationalism
Leadership
Learning
Listening
Openness
Passion
People-led
Pride
Principles
Professionalism
Progressiveness
Quality
Relevance
Reputation
Respect
Responsibility
Responsiveness
Sharing
Simplicity
Spirituality
Student-centred
Sustainability
Transformative
Transparency
Trust

www.ingramcontent.com/pod-product-compliance
Lightning Source LLC
Chambersburg PA
CBHW052343210326
41597CB00037B/6241